# ST. JOHN
## Feet, Fins & Four-Wheel Drive

**A complete guide to all of the island's
beaches, trails, and roads.**

### by Pam Gaffin

## Updated 2013

**American Paradise Publishing    St. John, USVI**

Cover by Keryn Bryan
Maps by Lee Stanciauskas


American Paradise Publishing
PO Box 781
St. John, VI 00831
Published 1994. Revised 2001. Reprinted with Updates 2003 and 2006,
Revised 2009, Reprinted with Update 2013.

# TABLE OF CONTENTS

# PREFACE

Back in 1994, I wrote *St. John: Feet, Fins & Four Wheel Drive* so that visitors would know how to get to someplace other than Trunk Bay, and for my friends to give to their guests when they couldn't take time off from work to be the tour guide. I wasn't sure how many people would really want to hike all the trails, snorkel all the beaches, and drive all the roads, rather than just spend their vacation sitting on the beach. Well, it turns out there are quite a few of you out there. Thank you all for making this book a success, and I hope you had and continue to have fun exploring.

Over the years, I have continually revised and updated *St. John: Feet, Fins & Four Wheel Drive* as the island grows and changes. No, the beaches haven't moved, the trails haven't changed much, and there aren't really any new roads, but we are no longer the sleepy little undiscovered place we use to be. (The latest updates can be found in the "Major Changes Since Last Update" chapter in the back of this book).

Some of the changes are good – the $1 public bus, the roundabout (traffic circle) in Cruz Bay, a third bank, gourmet supermarkets with fresh meat and vegetables, two bakeries, Internet access, two newspapers, and ATM machines (they don't always work). The long awaited Enighed Pond Cargo facility is finally open for barge traffic, and you may be able to use your cell phone (beware of extremely expensive roaming international charges from connecting with Tortola's tower).

Some are not so good: Overdevelopment is now a major problem. There is no longer a visually-pristine sandy beach bay – you can see at least one St. John house (if not dozens) from all of them. Even worse, it is not just enormous villas under construction everywhere; the high-density exploiters have discovered St. John. Our infrastructure cannot cope with the current population (there is a 3-year waiting list for a telephone line and water rationing every spring). How will it handle the massive increases in demand when these monstrosities are finished? Fortunately the 2009 financial crash stopped the developers cold for a few years, but now they are starting back up again.

Along with development, a number of other things are in a "wait and see what happens" pattern. There is promise of high speed Internet access to all three Virgin Islands. AT&T keeps promising they are going to upgrade our cell towers, some new gas stations are under construction but none are open yet, Maho Campground is on a year-to-year lease and may fold at any time. Cannel Bay has decided it does not like visitors or locals. These issues, along with other changes made since this book was revised in 2009, are detailed in the chapter "Major Changes Since Last Update."

Due to global warming, hurricanes have become a constant rather than a once-in-a-lifetime occurrence, and we are thoroughly sick of them. Global warming is also the cause of the 2005 Coral die-off – 50% of our coral died in that year. The water temperature got very high, causing coral bleaching, which weakened the corals so much that a virus killed half of our live coral in just a few months. It was and continues to be heartbreaking, but as a visitor you probably won't notice because St. John is still absolutely beautiful under the water and the corals are working overtime to grow back. Recently it was discovered that the coral in our mangroves were never affected by the 2005 die-off and are thriving in number and diversity.

Road paving is happening quite rapidly (for St. John). This is great news for the reefs since dirt roads pour tons of silt into the sea, smothering the coral and decreasing visibility. This does not eliminate the need for four-wheel drive vehicles but does decrease the need for expert off-road driving skills.

The hiking trails have improved. The Park managed to get funds to clear all of the trails at the same time and since then there have been enough of you regularly hiking to keep the path clear of brush – even on the long, difficult trails. Good job! There are even some new trails, courtesy of the "Trail Bandit" who spends his frequent visits to St. John clearing old Danish road beds with his machete. Back in the States, he creates very nice trail maps that he lets you download for free, or you can buy a printed map from him or from many of our local stores. He also offers downloadable GPS coordinates. The National Park folks hated him for a long time but happily, they have now reached an understanding of some kind. Contact Bob at www.TrailBandit.org.

Some things have not changed: Electricity and telephones still go out all the time, we never have enough water, there is nowhere to park in Cruz Bay, waiting in line forever at First Bank and post office continues to be the norm and the VI Government continues to say they are bankrupt.

St. John continues to have a spectacular selection of restaurants. Some restaurants started up, went broke and are now gone, but there always seems to be another person ready to try again. Of course, many restaurants are still around and still excellent – for example, La Tapa, The Lime Inn, Fish Trap, Morgan's Mango, Banana Deck, Shipwreck, Hercules, and Joe's BBQ.

People still stop their car in the middle of the road to talk to friends, the slower pace of "island time" still prevails, the price of rum is still dirt cheap, and entertainment is still basically a "do-it-yourself" proposition.

Other than a slight increase in people and houses on the hillsides, the beaches have not changed – powdery white sand, warm blue water, coconut trees swaying in the breeze, and some of the best snorkeling in the world.

In spite of the increase in population and complexity, St. John continues to be a very special place, and St. Johnians, very special, wonderful people. I am lucky to live here, and even luckier to have the opportunity to write about it. Thanks to all of the people who helped and encouraged me during the creation and revision of this book. I also want to thank all of the wonderful zany people who tour the island of St. John. Enjoy your vacation.

Once again, I have done my best to be accurate and I hope you will let me know where I failed. I also welcome your corrections, suggestions, and comments. Write Pam Gaffin, American Paradise Publishing, PO Box 781, St. John, VI 00831 or pam@AmericanParadisePublishing.com.

# WELCOME TO ST. JOHN

You've made it to the island – your long-awaited vacation in the American Paradise is about to begin. You're standing on the ferry dock or sitting on your balcony admiring the view. Now what?

St. John is not large, not too developed, not very populous, and not very sophisticated. If your idea of a dream vacation features glitzy nightlife, tons of shopping, noisy casinos, and lots of people – you are on the wrong island.

However, if you have arrived on St. John in search of natural beauty, friendly people, a vibrant community, and a pristine environment – then you are in *exactly* the right place.

Why? Because St. John is unique. It has a distinctly different history than St. Thomas, St. Croix, or Tortola. There are subtle reasons for this – cultural, tribal, geographic, and agricultural reasons. St. Johnians have always taken pride in their well-deserved reputation for being fiercely independent, self-sufficient, and community-minded. What other tiny tropic island would refer to its only town as 'Love City'?

Another reason St. John is so unique is because of the National Park. Over half the island falls within its protective boundaries. No other island in the Caribbean has expended so much money, time, talent, careful thought, and hard labor to ward off the corrosive influence of modern man.

You say you want beaches? There are 39 of them – big ones, little ones, crowded ones, and lonely ones. There are beaches for sunbathing, beaches for beachcombing, and beaches for snorkeling. We've got sandy bays, rocky bays, mangrove bays, and even salt ponds. There are beaches that are only two steps from your car, and beaches that you can only get to by hiking a long way. A few of our beaches have shops, snack bars, and facilities – but most are splendidly undeveloped and natural.

No matter how idealized your expectations of the 'perfect tropical beach' may be – we've got a beach which will meet or exceed them. Guaranteed.

Hiking? St. John has ten-minute and all-day trails, easy trails and rather hard trails – and trails to historic ruins, isolated beaches, and salt ponds teeming with birds. There are over 20 miles of trails just in The Park alone.

As for historic sites, there are ruins of five windmills on the island, old sugar cane factories, plantation Great Houses, mysterious petroglyphs, and even the landmarks of one of the most important slave insurrections in the world.

St. John roads snake alongside some of the most spectacular beaches in the world, and regularly offer breathtaking views of both the Caribbean Sea and the Atlantic Ocean.

Taxis are available to take you to some of the more popular beaches and the bus can take you across the island, but the best way to fully explore St. John is by rental jeep.

There are many curve-by-curve 'jeep tours' within this book, and one of them is just right for you, whether you're able to spend an active day or a leisurely month exploring the island.

We do, of course, have nightlife and shopping – and we certainly know how to party. Cruz Bay has a wide variety of shops, restaurants, and bars but you don't need a guidebook for that – just wander around town and enjoy. Wednesdays and Fridays are the biggest nights for live bands, but there's usually music somewhere on other nights. Special events, like a fish fry or benefit dance or baseball game or kite flying contest or historical lecture are advertised by posters all over town.

OK, now where are the beaches, the ruins, the protected forests and the trails? What should you do if you've only got one day? How can you get around the island?

That's what this book is for – to tell you what's out there, how to get to it, how to find it and how to enjoy it.

Welcome to St. John. Have fun exploring.

# GENERAL INFO

**St. John** is the smallest of the three main U.S. Virgin Islands. At latitude 18°20' and longitude 64°45', the island is about 4 miles east of St. Thomas and even closer to British Tortola. Rugged and mountainous, St. John (no it is not St. John's) is about 9 miles long and 5 miles across its widest point. It has a landmass of approximately 19 square miles. The **Arawak, Carib,** and **Taino** Indians were the original settlers of St. John. The Danes took possession of the Virgin Islands in 1694 and officially colonized St. John in 1717.

In spite of belonging to the Danes, the majority of settlers who homesteaded were Dutch. The Danish and Dutch planters had to clear the land, terrace the steep hillsides, and plant sugar cane. This was very hard work and soon killed off the Danish prisoners brought over to accomplish it. To fill the void in their labor force, the Danes imported slaves from Africa.

Even back then, St. John was the "poor cousin" to St. Thomas and St. Croix. The local planters of St. John could not afford to buy the "best" slaves (those who were most docile), so they ended up with the "troublemakers," those Africans unwilling to surrender their independence so easily. **Prince Aquashi** and **King Bolombo** (both noblemen in their native Africa) were two St. John slaves who refused to live in chains. They organized the other slaves and staged an island-wide revolt in 1733. They quickly massacred the European plantation families and held the island for six months against the best efforts of the Danes and the British. Only when hundreds of French troops were also brought in, were they finally defeated. Even then, the rebels refused to give up. Legend has it they instead chose mass suicide, jumping off cliffs into the sea (there is some debate on which cliffs – Mary's Point, Brown Bay, or Ram Head).

New planters arrived soon after the revolt and the plantations continued using slaves until the practice was legally abolished by Denmark in 1848. During this same period, sugar plantations throughout the Caribbean were experiencing severe competition from the new, fast-growing European sugar beet industry. The market price of sugar plummeted worldwide. A very strong hurricane hit St. John in 1867. This signaled the beginning of the end for many of the large-scale sugar plantations. The planters gradually began to drift away, abandoning their homes, investments, and responsibilities. During this time many of the freed slaves were able to acquire small tracts of land, either as gifts from the departing planters or by purchasing small parcels at reduced prices now that the boom was over.

In 1917 the **United States** purchased the Virgin Islands from **Denmark** for 24 million dollars ($300 an acre) in order to have a military base in the Caribbean. Today the **United States Virgin Islands** are a U.S. territory, which means we are U.S. citizens, hold U.S. passports, and pay U.S. income taxes. However, we can't vote for president (maybe it's time for a tea party?). We elect our local government which consists of a Governor, Lieutenant Governor, and 15 Senators, all of whom spend lots of money and have created an enormous deficit – just like in the good ole USA. The VI government is the largest employer in the islands and also boasts the most paid holidays for its employees – about 30 per year – of any island in the Caribbean. We have a representative in Washington, D.C., but she cannot vote in the House of Representatives.

In the 1950's Laurance Rockefeller 'discovered' St. John and purchased a huge chunk of it. He kept Caneel as a Rock Resort and donated about 5,000 acres to the federal government to establish the **Virgin Islands National Park.** The Park has added to this land over the years and now owns about 52% of the island.

The VI National Park boundaries now encompass almost three-quarters of the island, but there are numerous "in-holdings" (private land) that the Park hopes to eventually acquire. (Increased land values are now making this increasing unlikely.) In 1962, the Park borders were expanded to include 5,650 underwater acres (in some areas line fishing is permitted within Park waters; spear fishing is not. Water skiing and jet skiing are also prohibited. Traditional fishing with fish 'pots' is allowed).

After the plantations closed, the population of St. John was less than 1,000 for many years. In 1970 the population was 1,700. Today's population is about 4,500 permanent residents with a few hundred more part-timers (we call them snow birds) tossed in. Coral Bay was the main settlement on St. John up until about the 1950's when tourists arriving by ferry from St. Thomas caused Cruz Bay to become the main town.

The island is mainly of volcanic origin and is extremely hilly with deeply-etched valleys. This makes for lovely little scalloped bays and lots of beaches – more than 39 of them! Most of the land is at least a 20-degree slope, and the only flat portion is the small flood plain in Coral Bay. (It is not, thankfully, big enough to build a runway for planes.) For the most part, traveling around St. John consists of going up, down and around all these steep hills.

The climate is mild but dry. The year round average temperature is about 80 degrees. The average annual rainfall is 30-40 inches (most of that on the North side). There is no real rainy season, although normally it rains more during the peak of hurricane season in September and October. St. John has very little groundwater and – except for a very few businesses and houses right in Cruz Bay which have "city water" piped in, everyone relies on using their roofs to catch rainwater to fill their cisterns. Water is very expensive to buy, and not always available. So water conservation has become a fine art on St. John.

Hurricane Hugo in 1989, which was supposed to have been the "storm of the century," was the beginning of a 20-year cycle of intense storm activity. But the 20 years is up and now they say it is global warming causing the increased activity. Now tropical storms are a routine (but dreaded) part of summer and fall.

The vegetation is quite varied, depending on the amount of rain each area receives. The North Shore and Bordeaux Mountain areas get the most rain, so they have large woody trees. The very dry areas, like Salt Pond and the East End, have cactus and century plants. Mangrove swamps are found in Reef Bay, Fish Bay, Coral Bay, and Hurricane Hole. Elsewhere it is relatively dry.

Since St. John has always been an island, all the critters here had to either fly, swim, ride on floating coconuts, or be brought here by boat. The insects that made it here include sand flies, mosquitoes, bees, ants, and termites. Those huge, black, lumpy masses in the trees are termite nests. By the way, the large black centipedes are poisonous if eaten. These are not creatures that I would personally think of as standard dinner fare, but a 4-year-old friend of mine ate one and got extremely sick. He insists that I should warn everyone, so, of course, I must.

The only native mammals are five species of bats, which come out at night to eat bugs and fruit – no vampires here. Introduced mammals are rats, the mongooses that were brought to eat the rats (someone neglected to do their homework on this one since rats are nocturnal and mongooses aren't), and donkeys brought as pack animals. St. John has no large predators, so the mongoose population has exploded (a mongoose looks like a squirrel that forgot to curl his tail). Since the donkeys were let loose after being replaced by cars, they too have survived nicely. Both have learned how to steal picnic lunches.

Now that it is possible and easy to buy meat on St. John, domestic goats that have gone wild are abundant because no one can be bothered to hunt them. Large numbers of goats are now roaming all over the island causing tremendous amounts of erosion. The feral cat population is finally under control thanks to the hard work of our vets and the **Animal Care Center** volunteers who capture and neuter/spay the animals. Maybe they can start working on the goats?

There are also a few wild boars that are almost impossible to get to see. Our deer population has increased so that they are now fairly easy to find. Very easy to spot are the lizards, six different kinds, which will consume all the mosquitoes and bugs in your room if you leave them alone (they don't hurt humans). Most of the lizards like to do push-ups, which is supposed to scare off threatening things, like you, so please act scared.

There are some Common Iguanas, but very few because the mongooses eat their eggs. Another interesting creature to watch is a land crab with red legs, the Soldier or Hermit Crab. They live in discarded shells, usually whelk, and make an amazing amount of noise when they are walking through the woods or rummaging under your house at sunset looking for dinner. These little guys can really get around. They can go straight up cement walls or trees, and nothing stops them when they do their annual migration down to the sea in August to breed. The soldier crabs are harmless to humans unless you pick them up wrong. Then they reach around with that big claw, grab you and don't let go easily. They are also excellent pot scrubbers. If the stew got cooked a little too long, put the pot out at night. The crabs will clean off all the baked-on stuff by morning.

The **St. John Audubon Society** or the National Park can help you with detailed information on birds. We have lots of **hummingbirds, banana quits, doves,** and **thrushies** (also good at stealing lunches). Many (trendy) North American birds winter here. Sea birds include **pelicans, boobies, terns,** and the ever-present **seagulls.** One bird found frequently in the trees might surprise you; St. John chickens fly pretty well "cause the dogs can't get them up in the trees."

The most abundant wildlife on St. John is found underwater. The bays are teeming with colorful **fish, anemones,** hard and soft **corals, sponges, lobsters, squid, octopuses, shrimp, starfish, eels, urchins, rays, conch, turtles** and more. Visiting St. John without going snorkeling is like going to the Grand Canyon and not looking over the edge.

The National Park has instituted a policy to exterminate or minimize "exotic species" of plants and animals. Their definition of "indigenous" is anything before Columbus (the 1400's). Using this definition, all mammals except bats are "exotic" – boar, deer, donkeys, mongoose, rats, mice, cats, dogs, goats, cows. Federal hunters have been brought to St John to trap and/or kill the "exotic animals." "Exotic" plants include most of the fruit trees (including coconut palms), and many of the plants eaten by grazing animals. A botanist was brought to St. John to experiment by spraying poison in some areas of the park, killing a selection of "exotics" then trying to replant with "indigenous" species. The Park acknowledges that it will be impossible to completely eradicate the "exotic" plants and animals since they do not own the entire island. But they are content to just "do the best they can" to contain as much as possible the "exotics." I remind them that using their definition, Park Rangers are also "exotic."

The **National Park Visitors Center** and some of the gift shops have excellent books about the history, geology, plants, fauna, and underwater life of St. John. The Park also has an excellent map of the island (free), which I highly recommend.

There is one other important natural treasure on St. John – **the people.** The island's population consists of native Virgin Islanders, a large number of "down islanders," a Spanish-speaking population from the Dominican Republic and Puerto Rico, and "continentals." With a relatively small population, it's easy for everyone to know each other. People are recognized by the car they drive, and everyone takes time to talk to each other in the streets (sometimes blocking traffic).

We have what may be considered old-fashioned customs, like greeting everyone with a "good morning," "good afternoon," or expecting your body to be covered up when not on the beach (you can actually get a ticket for walking around Cruz Bay in your bathing suit).

# WHAT IS WHERE?

St. John is not very big – so how hard can it be to find something? Sometimes pretty hard. The free official Virgin Islands Government road map, which is sometimes available at the Tourist Information Bureau, is not extremely useful. The map shows a large number of paved roads which do not exist except as goat trails (routes 204, 103, 20 going into Coral Bay, 109, 107 going from Bordeaux to Lameshur), some that do exist but are difficult, unpaved dirt roads (105, 206,107 from Salt Pond to Lameshur, 108) and yet it doesn't show a major road, which actually exists, at all (Fish Bay Road).

The very best map available is the **VI National Park map.** This map also shows two roads that are actually goat trails (route 204 from Centerline near Gift Hill to North Shore Road, and a road from Centerline near the North Shore Road intersection straight down to Coral Bay). Both these roads have not been maintained in years and have large washed-out sections. They are completely impassable by vehicle and very dangerous.

The free, blue-colored **St. John Map** distributed by Great Dane is pretty good but doesn't contain a lot of detail. But the biggest problem is that the island is so small that we all know where everything is and just assume that you do too. Sometimes it may seem like we are talking in secret code, but there is a method to our madness.

"Town" is Cruz Bay, the main community where the ferries come in. Coral Bay, the small settlement on the other side of the island is never "town," it's just Coral Bay. In town, street names, if they ever had a name, are totally unused. Forget about building numbers – they don't exist.

Instead, landmarks are used to describe the street. We usually use a business that is fairly conspicuous. In Cruz Bay the important reference points are: the Dock, the Park, First Bank, Connections, Mongoose Junction, National Park Visitors Center, Wharfside Village, the Roundabout (where the Texaco Gas

Station used to be) and the Boulon Center.

The few main roads on the island are referred to by name. The maps of St. John do show route numbers. If you are paying close attention, you might spot 1 or 2 signs around the island using these numbers. But only map makers and tourists ever pay any attention to them. If you ask for directions using a route number, no one will know what you are talking about. They will probably think you are crazy. Occasionally you might spot some milepost markers, which are not used because no one knows where they were started from, and because there are so few of them. (Recently, the road crews went out and re-measured the roads and installed new mileposts, but they did not bother to take down all the old ones. Plus, they still seem to be measuring from some unknown point).

The National Park finally put up some signs identifying major beaches and trails but if (when) they are blown down in the next storm or knocked out by a car or stolen by some idiot, do not expect them to be replaced promptly (remember, it took over 40 years for the first set of signs to be put up).

For the road tours in this book, I have given mileage readings that start from obvious reference points. I've also attempted to give you useful descriptions of recognizable landmarks which are helpful in locating different beaches, trails, and ruins.

It's pretty hard to get lost, just keep driving and you'll end up either in Cruz Bay, Coral Bay, or at the end of the road.

The names of the main roads on the island are: Centerline Road, North Shore Road, Gift Hill Road, South Shore Road, Fish Bay Road, Salt Pond Road, Lameshur Road and East End Road. The Westin is located on the South Shore Road, Caneel Bay Resort and Cinnamon Bay Campground are on the North Shore Road, Maho Bay Campground is just off of the North Shore Road, and Concordia Resort is on Salt Pond Road.

The side roads off the main road sometimes have names, but usually are described by someone who lives on them or by an obvious landmark (the road across from Cable TV). This may seem confusing, but it does work. Using this method, one house address is "on Gift Hill, down the road Miss Stella lived on, the house where the horses used to live" (Note: the horses moved out over 10 years ago). Believe it or not, the propane gas deliveryman would know exactly where that is.

## CRUZ BAY

Cruz Bay is the "big city," with the police station, fire station, two banks, the post office, some government offices, and a gas station.

The best way to explore Cruz Bay is to start wandering around, stopping in whatever shops, bars, or restaurants that strike your fancy. The whole town consists of only a few streets. Nothing is more than a five-minute walk away, so it's pretty hard to get lost. (Except that some people end up past the Roundabout still looking for "downtown;" they can't believe they already went through it).

There are public bathrooms located by the big parking lot near the Customs Building. The public toilets at the National Park Visitors Center are usually closed and best avoided even if they are open.

The VI Government has a Tourist Information office, but it is difficult to find. It is hidden in the small space between the Post Office and the old clinic and Sparky's (now called Captains Quarters) in the park. There is only a small sign on the door, and since the door is always closed to keep the air conditioning in, it is hard to tell whether it's open or not (official hours are Monday through Friday from 8-5, closed on holidays). Former employees seemed to like being invisible, but now we have Lucinda who really wants tourists to find the office, and who has lots of good information to pass along once they get there. She is working on getting more signs up, and hosts different events in the small park area out front (music, crafts demonstrations, etc.). The picnic table under the shady tree is a good place to take a break when you are wandering around town.

An alternate source of tourist information is **Connections,** located diagonally across from First Bank. These wonderful ladies know everything there is to know about St. John, and a whole lot more. In addition to answering questions, they do bookings for day sail and fishing charters, long distance calls, faxes, photocopies, typing, notary documents, Western Union money transfers, phone cards, and Internet access.

Cruz Bay harbor has a large live-aboard boat population and lots of visiting yachts anchored within its confines. These boats, combined with the constant ferry traffic, make swimming or snorkeling in Cruz Bay uninviting. The reef that juts out from the left side (south) of the bay near the cemetery, offers good snorkeling if you don't mind all the boats zooming dangerously close by. In any event, the sandy beach between 'town' and the cemetery is great for walking or wading.

Parking is at a premium in town, especially during the day. Our police regularly give out parking tickets (which will get charged to your credit card by the car rental companies if you leave the island without paying it). The large public parking lot is almost always filled to capacity by our St. Thomas commuters during weekdays. Another parking area is next to Nature's Nook, but it, too, is used by all-day parkers. All of the parking places along the water by the dock are taken by taxis and the rest of the spots around town in front of different businesses are usually full (but you might get lucky). The public parking lot by the tennis courts is probably the only place that will have room for you during the day. This is not a great place to be parked at night, but by then all the other parking areas will be unoccupied. Check to see if whoever you rented a jeep from will allow you to park in their yard.

St. John currently has only one gas station open. In Cruz Bay, **E&C Gas** is on the Southshore Road at the bottom of Jacob's Ladder across from the basketball courts. In Coral Bay, the Domino Gas on Salt Pond Road between the Triangle and the dumpsters has been closed for a while but may open sometime soon. NOTE: E&C gas station is open from 7:00 am-8:00 pm Monday through Saturday, and from 7:00 am- 4:00 pm on Sunday and may be closed on holidays, including local holidays that may catch you by surprise.

Our banks have ATM machines that work most of the time, but do not wait until the last minute to get money, especially on holidays, because the machine may be out of cash and you will be stuck. There are a few ATM machines in businesses around the island, but these come and go – I'm not sure why. If you see a working one during your visit, great, but don't count on it being there in the future.

Most of the island's grocery stores are here in town: **Dolphin** and **Starfish Markets.** Outside of town on the South Shore Road are **Pine Peace Market,** and **St. John Market. Love City Mini Mart** and **Lily's Market** are in Coral Bay.

## THE NEW ROUNDABOUT (FORMERLY THE TEXACO GAS STATION INTERSECTION)

I am taking a huge leap of faith by calling this section the Roundabout because at the moment there isn't one – it is under construction and would be more accurately called "the large messy construction site surrounded by orange traffic cones." This construction is necessary to allow trucks to make it through the intersection without having to back up – which causes some truly spectacular traffic jams. However, no one really has any idea how it is all going to work out in the end (if it is ever finished), so I will just try to describe it the best I can.

This is where all the roads come together (5 of them!). Cars seem to come from all directions and if it was difficult to know who had the right of way before the construction chaos, it is even harder now. The best way to tackle this intersection is to yield, and then slowly go on while being ready to stop if someone else isn't going to.

As you come out of "downtown" Cruz Bay, the Y-shaped intersection splits with Centerline Road on the left and South Shore Road on the right. Within a few yards, Centerline Road intersects with the road leading to the Boulon Center, down to the North Shore Road. Within a few yards on the South Shore Road side, it intersects with the road going down to the fire station, the tennis court parking area, and over to the cargo dock. This road is the one-way portion of the South Shore Road when you are coming back into town.

To make things even more confusing, the construction forces various lanes and roads to be blocked off at various times, and different detours have to be made. Everyone is taking bets on when the system will completely break down and total gridlock will occur. So far, the traffic has continued to move, slowly, with great confusion, but it has moved. Keep your fingers crossed.


## THE ROADS

### CENTERLINE ROAD (ROUTE 10)

Centerline Road goes through the center of the island from Cruz Bay to Coral Bay and beyond, to the very end of the island – East End. In 1992 this road was resurfaced (long overdue) at a cost of about 7 million dollars. Even though this seems to be an awful lot of money to resurface just 13 miles of existing road, we are all grateful. Now it is possible to get from Cruz Bay to Coral Bay in 25 to 30 minutes – before it took 40 -50 minutes to go 7 ½ miles!

Only the maps consider the entire road from Cruz Bay to East End to be the same road. Everyone else talks of Centerline Road as going to Coral Bay, then from there out to the East End is called the East End Road. There are no beaches on Centerline; it runs along the ridge top of all the hills, offering excellent views of the sea. Trails starting on Centerline are: Water Catchment Trail, Margaret Hill Trail, Cinnamon Bay Trail, and Reef Bay Trail.

## NORTH SHORE ROAD (ROUTE 20)

North Shore Road starts in Cruz Bay, then enters the National Park and follows the north shore passing all the beautiful beaches to the Annaberg Ruins, then swings up the hill to connect with Centerline Road. At Annaberg, the road splits, one-way to Francis Bay and Maho Bay Campground, the other to Annaberg Ruins and Waterlemon Beach. This road is maintained by the Federal Government, which means it is always in much better shape than any of our other roads. All of the scenic overlooks are on the left side of the road so the best way to go sightseeing is to start from town and head towards Annaberg, not the other way. Most of St. John's best beaches are on the North Shore Road: Hawksnest Beach, Gibney's Beach, Jumbie Beach, Trunk Bay Beach, Peter Bay Beach, Cinnamon Bay Beach, Maho Bay Beach, Francis Bay Beach, and Waterlemon Beach.

Caneel Bay Resort, Cinnamon Bay Campground, and Maho Bay Campground are on this road.

Trails from the North Shore Road are: Lind Point Trail, Caneel Hill Trail, Margaret Hill Trail, Water Catchment Trail, Peace Hill Trail, Cinnamon Bay Nature Trail, Cinnamon Bay Trail, America Hill Trail, Maho Goat Trail, Mary's Point Schoolhouse Trail, Francis Bay Trail, Leinster Bay Trail, Brown Bay Trail, and Johnny Horn Trail.

Most of the plantation ruins and historic sites can be seen on the North Shore Road. Ruins are at: Caneel Bay, Peace Hill, Cinnamon Bay, the School House, Annaberg, behind Waterlemon beach, the old Boys Home on the Johnny Horn Trail, Frederiksdahl. The National Park Headquarters has an excellent Historic Map and Guide ($2.50), **"Danish St. Jon."**

## SOUTH SHORE ROAD AND GIFT HILL ROAD (ROUTE 104)

The mapmakers consider this as one road, but it is actually two. The South Shore Road starts at the Roundabout in Cruz Bay where it splits into two one-way streets, comes back together at the new sewage treatment plant corner, goes past the Marketplace and Starfish Market, then up Jacob's Ladder, past the Westin Hotel, and ends at the intersection of Gift Hill Road and Fish Bay Road. Gift Hill Road starts from there, climbing very steeply up to the top of Gift Hill and connecting with Centerline Road by the dump. The South Shore Road is a bit inland from the coast, so the beaches are a short way down side roads. They are: Great Cruz Bay Beach, Chocolate Hole Beach, Hart Bay Beach and Monte Bay

Beach. There are no beaches on Gift Hill Road and no trails on either road.

Here's how to successfully navigate the one-way-street confusion at the beginning of this road: coming out of town, take the right fork at the Roundabout and go straight on this narrow one-way road past Kilroy's Dry Cleaners, the Inn at Tamarind Court and a Laundromat. At the sewage treatment plant corner, go straight – you are now on a two-way road (if you turned right, you would end up back in town again). Coming from the South Shore Road, you will be forced to turn left at the sewage treatment plant corner. The road follows the salt pond and at the tennis courts makes a 90 degree turn to the right, goes up the hill over a speed hump past the fire station to a stop sign at the Roundabout. Go right to go back to the South Shore Road, go left to go everywhere else.

### SALT POND ROAD (ROUTE 107)

Salt Pond Road starts at the Triangle in Coral Bay and follows the shoreline until the Salt Pond parking lot, where it continues a little more going towards Lameshur Bay, and in the process becomes known as Lameshur Road. The VI Government finally paid the contractor so Salt Pond Road is now completely repaved, with new drainage and shiny new guardrails (we didn't get stuck with the rusty ones this time).

The terrible hill on Lameshur Road is paved!!! The rest of the road on both sides of the hill is still unpaved and you may still need four-wheel drive to negotiate it. Some of the rental car companies still prohibit their cars from using this road, but many people choose to ignore this rule. It is possible to walk to Lameshur but that hill is steep, so bring lots of water.

Beaches which are accessed by this road are: Johnson Bay Beach, Friis Bay Beach, Salt Pond Bay Beach, Drunk Bay Beach, Ram Head Trail Beach, Great Lameshur Beach, Little Lameshur Beach, and Europa Bay Beach.

Trails are: Drunk Bay Trail, Ram Head Trail, Bordeaux Mountain Trail, Lameshur Trail, and Europa Bay Trail.

### EAST END ROAD (CONTINUATION OF ROUTE 10)

Starting from the Coral Bay Triangle, the East End Road goes through "downtown" Coral Bay to the East End. It eventually turns into a dirt road, which takes you to the "end" of St. John. Only a small section of the road goes through the National Park. Beaches along the way are: Princess Bay Beach, Haulover North, Haulover South, Hansen Bay Beach, Long Bay Beach, Privateer Beach. Trails are: Johnny Horn Trail, Brown Bay Trail.

### FISH BAY ROAD (NOT ACKNOWLEDGED AS EXISTING, SO IT HAS NO ROUTE NUMBER)

Fish Bay Road is now almost all paved. It runs from the corner of South Shore and Gift Hill Roads, past Rendezvous Bay, down into the mangroves and the Fish Bay residential area, then over the hill to the Reef Bay side. If you are capable of scrambling over slippery boulders, the Little Reef Bay Trail can be used to get from Fish Bay over to the Reef Bay Trail.

Beaches accessed by this road are: Klein Bay Beach, both Dittlif Point Beaches, and Parret Bay Beach. Trails are: Dittlif Point Trail and Little Reef Bay Trail.

## BORDEAUX MOUNTAIN ROAD (ROUTE 108)

Bordeaux Mountain Road runs from the Centerline Road along the crest of the mountains to the peak of Bordeaux Mountain, then steeply down into Coral Bay. It is paved from Centerline Road to just past the Y-intersection. After that, the dirt road is usually passable as far as the Bordeaux Mountain Trailhead and a little further. BUT the down/down/down section has not received attention in years and usually is very close to being impassable – even with four-wheel drive. It is a terrifying collection of very steep grades, amazing switchbacks, and three-foot-deep washed-out ruts. It makes a far better hiking trail than it does a road. The VI Government is talking about paving it (maybe to catch up with their official map), but who knows when, if ever, that will actually happen. There are no beaches along this road. Trails are: the Bordeaux Mountain Trail.

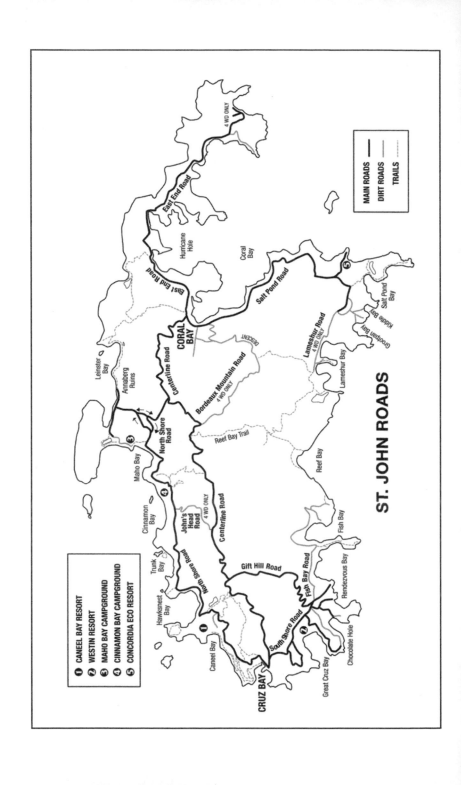

ST. JOHN ROADS

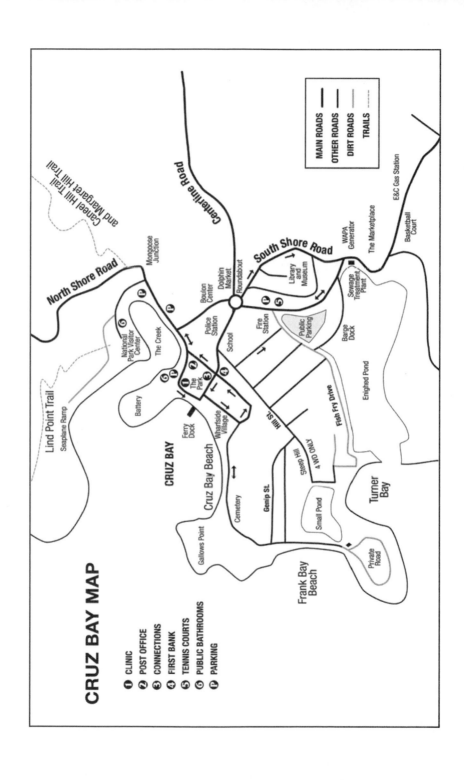

# CRUZ BAY MAP

1 CLINIC
2 POST OFFICE
3 CONNECTIONS
4 FIRST BANK
5 TENNIS COURTS
6 PUBLIC BATHROOMS
P PARKING

MAIN ROADS
OTHER ROADS
DIRT ROADS
TRAILS

North Shore Road
Centerline Road
South Shore Road

Caneel Hill Trail and Margaret Hill Trail
Mongoose Junction
Lind Point Trail
Seaplane Ramp
National Park Visitor Center
The Creek
Battery
Ferry Dock
Wharfside Village
The Park
Police Station
School
Fire Station
Boulon Center
Dolphin Market
Roundabout
Library and Museum
WAPA Generator
The Marketplace
Basketball Court
E&C Gas Station
Sewage Treatment Plant
Barge Dock
Public Parking
Enighed Pond
Fish Fry Drive
4 WD ONLY
Steep Hill
Mill St.
Genip St.
Cemetery
Gallows Point
Cruz Bay Beach
CRUZ BAY
Small Pond
Frank Bay Beach
Turner Bay
Private Road

# GETTING AROUND

Your choices on how to get around the island are: take the bus (has a limited route), take a taxi (also has limited routes), walk (lots of steep hills in tropical heat), or rent a jeep (expensive).

## THE BUS
St. John finally has a public transportation system. It is terrific and hopefully it is going to last a long time (so far it has survived a few budget cuts, keep your fingers crossed). The buses run most of the time and are one of the island's best (only?) bargains – $1 to go from the Cruz Bay ferry dock all the way out to Salt Pond! The bus leaves the ferry dock at about 20 to 25 minutes after the hour. It travels across Centerline Road to Coral Bay, goes straight past Skinny Legs to the Flamingo Club. Here it turns around and goes back to the Coral Bay Triangle, takes a left onto Salt Pond Road and keeps going all the way to the parking lot at Salt Pond. It generally leaves Salt Pond to begin the return trip at 10 minutes after the hour, gets to the Coral Bay Triangle at about 15 minutes past the hour, and makes it back to the ferry dock just before the top of the hour (so you can make the ferry).

There are very few official bus stops. Simply stand in a safe spot for the bus to stop (not on a curve) and flag it down. Ask the bus driver for his/her guess as to what time to wait for the return bus. The price is one dollar for any distance and you must have exact change. The bus runs from about 5 am to 7 pm. Make sure you do not miss the last bus! The St. John folks in charge of the buses do a spectacular job in spite of their boss – the chronically broke and incredibly inefficient VI Government. But they cannot perform miracles, so do not be surprised to discover that all of the buses are not running or that they are not on time – that way you might be pleasantly surprised rather than badly disappointed. Call 776-6346 for up-to-date information about the buses.

The bus primarily exists for locals to get to and from work, not for tourists to have a cheap island tour (sorry). Therefore, it does not go to the fabulous North Shore beaches, or to Annaberg, or to any of the hotels, but it can take you to Salt Pond Beach and a number of trails (Water Catchment Trail, Cinnamon Bay Trail, Reef Bay Trail, Johnny Horn Trail).

## TAXIS

Although there are some taxi drivers who will take you anywhere on St. John, many of our taxi drivers will only go to a limited number of places – usually to and from the hotels and along the North Shore Road as far as Cinnamon Bay. (I know taxis are supposed to take you where *you* want to go, but here many of them will only go where *they* want to go). Each hotel and campground has its own taxis to take you to and from town and to some North Shore beaches. They may also offer island tours and possibly special trips out to Coral Bay or Salt Pond Beach.

The taxi fleet in Cruz Bay exists primarily to transport large tour groups. Taxi fares are based on the number of people carried, not on one price to go to a destination. This explains why drivers are more interested in taking a full load of 25 cruise ship passengers to Trunk Bay than they are in taking 2 people to the Reef Bay Trail. The larger your group, the larger your chances are of finding a taxi to where you want to go (of course, with a large group it may be cheaper to rent a car).

The taxi association will give you an island tour – North Shore Road, Annaberg and back via Centerline Road, but they usually don't do beach stops on the tour unless you work out a special deal.

## WALK

It is possible to walk. There are a number of beaches and trails accessible on foot from Cruz Bay. Those resorts on the North Shore – Caneel Bay, Cinnamon Bay Campground, and Maho Bay Campground are also within walking distance of other beaches and trailheads.

For those people who enjoy walking or even running longer distances, I can recommend the **8 Tuff Miles** race that is held every year in February. This very popular race from Cruz Bay to Coral Bay along Centerline Road has grown over the years and now involves over 700 people – about 100 serious athletic competitors, about 100 normal people of all ages out for a nice stroll, and the rest something in between. The serious folks can run this route in an hour; my parents (mid-sixties) and I walked it in three hours (we stopped for ice cream along the way) to win the Lead Foot award for being dead last. The race is a community fundraiser and a lot of fun. Contact www.8TuffMiles.com for details. Of course, you don't have to wait for the race; it is a great hike anytime.

## RENT A JEEP

The best way to get around is to rent a jeep, at least for 1 or 2 days. Then you can go where you want, when you want, and are not limited to the North Shore Road. Plus, a rental jeep is the only way to do any of the road trips in this book.

## NORTH SHORE ROAD DESTINATIONS

The Lind Point Trail leading to Salomon, Honeymoon, and Caneel Bay beaches starts in Cruz Bay, as do the Caneel Hill and Margaret Hill trails. The bus does not run along this road. Taxis will happily take you to Caneel Bay Resort and all along the North Shore Road as far as Cinnamon Bay Campground. They will drop you off at any beach and make arrangements to pick you up at a certain time. Since there is plenty of taxi traffic on this road, you could easily flag one down when you are ready leave rather than having to decide on a time in advance. Past Cinnamon Bay, you might be able to find a taxi to take you as far as Annaberg, but if not, Maho Bay Campground has its own shuttle that leaves Cruz Bay at regular set times and goes along the entire length of the North Shore Road. It will drop you off along the way. Ask the taxi drivers at the dock what the current schedule is if you want to get to Maho Beach, Little Maho, Francis Bay Beach and Trail, Annaberg Ruins or Waterlemon Beach and the Leinster Bay, Johnny Horn and Brown Bay Trails.

## CENTERLINE ROAD AND BORDEAUX MOUNTAIN ROAD DESTINATIONS

Centerline Road crosses the length of the island from Cruz Bay to Coral Bay. The bus runs along this road, but it is not easy to get a taxi to go on Centerline. You might find a taxi that will drop you off at the Water Catchment and Margaret Hill Trails, since that's not too far out of town. Past that, to get to the Catherineberg Ruins, the Cinnamon Bay Trail, the Reef Bay Trail, and to Chateaux Bordeaux it gets harder but is still possible. From Bordeaux on to Coral Bay is almost impossible; you need to rent a jeep, or take the bus. The hotels and campgrounds may have an organized tour to go to the Reef Bay Trail. If not, the National Park does have one, once or twice a week, that includes transport from Cruz Bay to the trail and a boat ride back to town. (Sign up well in advance.) No taxi will go down Bordeaux Mountain Road, but you could walk from Chateau Bordeaux to the Bordeaux Mountain Trail.

## SALT POND ROAD AND LAMESHUR DESTINATION

You can take the bus to Salt Pond but it will not go to Lameshur. Your best bet is to rent a jeep to get to these areas. The majority of our taxi divers will not take one or two people out to Coral Bay, never mind to Salt Pond. No regular taxi will go to Lameshur since it is a four-wheel drive (4WD) only dirt road. The hotels might offer a tour to Salt Pond, (Maho Bay Campground has regularly scheduled ones to both Salt Pond and Lameshur that anyone can join, but you need to get out to Maho).

Hitchhiking is possible but we don't officially recommend it. Occasionally hitchhikers have been ripped off, and/or assaulted in the Virgin Islands. It's rare, but it does happen. Don't chance it. (If you insist on hitchhiking, remember that in St. John you to stick your index finger out in the direction you want to go, not your thumb). To hitch from Cruz Bay out to Salt Pond will take a long time.

## EAST END ROAD DESTINATIONS

Again you are going to need a rental car/jeep. The bus doesn't go there, very few taxis go out to the East End, and there are not very many people living out there so hitchhiking is very difficult.

## SOUTH SHORE ROAD AND FISH BAY ROAD DESTINATIONS

Cruz Bay Beach, Frank Bay, and Turner Bay are all within easy walking distance of Cruz Bay. Taxis will happily take you from Cruz Bay to the Westin at Great Cruz Bay, but are reluctant to go much beyond that point to Chocolate Hole and Hart Bay unless you have a large group. Taxis will seldom go on the Fish Bay Road.

## GIFT HILL ROAD

There are no major tourist destinations on this road, so taxis don't usually like to go this way. You might convince a taxi to take this road instead of Centerline to or from certain destinations, for example from the Westin to the Reef Bay Trail.

## ST. JOHN BY SEA

Another way to get around St. John is by sea. Most of the hotels, campgrounds, and guesthouses offer full or half-day sails, which include snorkeling stops. Some of the faster boats (catamarans and power boats) offer an **Around St. John** trip with 3 or more snorkeling stops. This is a great way to see the island and get to snorkel spots not accessible by land. Contact **Connections** (Tel. 776-6922) to book these trips.

Small power boats and inflatable dinghies can be rented if you want to do your own tour: contact **Ocean Runner** (Tel. 693-8809), **Noah's Little Arks** (Tel. 693-9030), or **Crabby's** in Coral Bay (Tel.714-2415).

Scuba diving is another way to explore St. John. There are dive operators at the Westin, Caneel, Cinnamon Bay, and Maho Bay, or the two dive companies in Cruz Bay – **Low Key Watersports** (Tel. 693-8999) and **Cruz Bay Watersports** (Tel. 776-6234).

Sea Kayaks are a fun way to get over to the uninhabited cays. Kayak tours or rentals are available at Maho Bay Campground, Cinnamon Bay Campground, Arawak Tours (Tel. 693-8313), or Crabby's in Coral Bay (Tel. 714-2415) or my favorite, Hidden Reef Eco-Tours (877-529-2575).

# THE BEACHES

## HOW TO SUN, SWIM, AND SNORKEL

St. John has lots and lots of beaches and the crystal clear water is warm all year round. Most of the beaches are white sand, with palm trees for shade, waves about 2 inches high, no drop-off, and at least one reef not too far out – ideal for sunbathing, swimming and snorkeling.

One of the few good things about St. John's lack of rainfall is that there is very little runoff from the mountains to muddy up the visibility in the sea. That incredible blue color of the water is from the sun reflecting off the white sandy bottom with nothing except fish to block the light beams. The darker blue areas are reefs or rocks. The fine dazzling white sand is from the coral itself. Some of it is made as the reefs erode, but much of the sand is courtesy of the parrotfish, who munch on hunks of coral, digest the algae from it, and then discharge the waste as sand. According to a Fish and Wildlife scientist, one parrotfish can produce up to 500 pounds of sand per year.

Beaches at many of the hotels and campgrounds offer snorkel rentals, chairs and floats, and refreshments. Trunk Bay Beach has snorkel and beach chair rentals and a snack bar. For the rest of the beaches, you have to bring your own water toys, suntan lotion, food and drinks.

The sun is tropical strength here, and even if you are from Florida it's stronger than you're use to. Use sunscreen and T-shirts to keep yourself unexposed and a hat that will keep you from getting fried brains (sunstroke). You may get sunburned in new places – favorite spots to forget in the greasing up process are your ears and your feet. SPF factors less than 30 are not even worth putting on. Almost all the beaches have trees to hide under to escape the sun. Wearing a T-shirt in the water will help prolong your swimming and snorkeling time.

Bring plenty of drinks. That sun will still dehydrate you even when you are not sweating. You'll lose fluids even while swimming. Bring twice as much liquid as you think you'll need. Alcoholic beverages speed up the dehydration process, so make sure you have some water, juice, or soda along too.

Donkeys, mongooses, and thrushie birds are common visitors to the beaches. They know all about tourists and especially about lunches. Keep your food in something they can't tear into and/or hang it as high in a tree as you can reach. Unfortunately, we also have a small number of human thieves on the island. Don't bring valuables to the beach and don't leave them in your rental car. It's best to leave them back at the hotel.

Feeding the animals and fish is prohibited. The donkeys got so used to people as a food source, that they started biting and kicking if you didn't feed them. Before Hurricane Hugo dispersed them, there was an unruly mob of stingrays at Honeymoon beach who were so spoiled that if you just stuck your toe in the water, you would be instantly surrounded by far too many stingrays looking for a handout.

At all National Park Beaches, everything is protected. This means you can't take home any souvenir shells, coral, rocks, or sand. Take as many pictures as you want (have you tried those nifty disposable underwater cameras?). Garbage belongs in a trash barrel. No, that nice white sand is not an ashtray.

In the water, don't stand on anything except sand. The reefs are fragile: the overachievers in the coral world can only produce an inch or so of new reef per year – most produce a half inch or less. The oil from your fingers is enough to smother live coral and a large foot or flailing flipper can destroy years of coral growth. As an extra incentive to be careful, we have sea urchins and fire coral, which fight back. Keep your feet and hands off the rocks and coral.

St. John is truly a snorkeler's paradise: most of the 39 accessible beaches have at least one reef nearby. Those beaches that don't have reefs have turtle grass or mangroves, which are also exciting to see. Only very few of the beaches are unsuitable for snorkeling.

There are lots of fish to see. They are easy to spot, even for beginners. (There are fish right at the shoreline, in 6 inches of water!)

Snorkeling requires an ability to swim, some practice using the gear, a sensible assessment of your physical condition, and some common sense.

Common problems for snorkelers are: too tired to get back from wherever they got to, trouble in deep water because they didn't practice long enough in the shallow water, and injuries because they didn't keep their hands and feet off the rocks and coral.

The most common injuries to snorkelers are sunburn, coral scrapes which become infected, fire coral burns, or contact with a sea urchin's long black spines. All of these can be prevented if you wear a T-shirt and never touch or stand on anything except sand.

The wildlife underwater will see you as a large predator and will not bother you unless you threaten them. Sticking your fingers in holes is threatening to the moray eel that lives there, and he will defend himself. Using a stick to poke at something is also a good way to provoke a defensive attack.

Another way to upset the normal underwater routine is to feed the fish. You will alter their feeding habits, which may cause unusual aggressive behavior in the fish. Be content to watch and look. It is safer to be a spectator rather than an active participant in the food chain.

Snorkel gear can be rented from the hotels and campgrounds, or from the dive shops.

# SNORKEL LESSON

One of my jobs was to take huge mobs of cruise ship passengers to Trunk Bay and quickly teach them how to snorkel. So here's my well-tested snorkeling lesson for those of you who have never snorkeled, or haven't done it in a long time, or always have problems with a leaky mask.

The secret to snorkeling successfully is to have a mask that doesn't leak. The way that a mask keeps the water out is that every bit of the inside edge has to seal perfectly to your skin; greasy suntan lotion or even a small piece of hair will ruin the seal. Faces come in different shapes and sizes, and, thus, so do masks. (Forget what the outside looks like, it's the inner seal that's important.)

There is a way to know before you get in the water whether or not your mask fits. Without using the strap, put the mask on your face, inhale through your nose, and do "no hands." The mask should stick to your face as long as you are inhaling. If it won't stick, try another shaped mask. People with moustaches are handicapped individuals in this sport – try to shove the mask as far up under your nose as you can, in order to find that little bit of skin for the mask to seal to. Vaseline, lip balm, or peanut butter can be used on your moustache to make it seal better.

Once you have passed this test, the only way your mask can leak is if you are doing one of two things. 1) Exhaling through your nose – when you exhale through your nose, it breaks the seal and water can come in. 2) Laughing – when you laugh your check bones move and your forehead might wiggle, breaking the seal and letting water come in.

The strap is only there to keep the mask from falling off your head. Tightening the strap will not make the mask stop leaking; only the right mask for your face can do that. The strap should be tight enough to keep the mask from wiggling around, but not so tight that you get a headache. For some reason, everyone seems to like to wear the strap down around their ears. This hurts. You don't need to be in pain to snorkel. Also, a strap in this position keeps pulling the mask down off your face. Place the strap on the crown of your head, up high.

To keep your mask from fogging up you need to use some anti-fog. The best stuff to use is your spit – there is some kind of chemical in your saliva that de-fogs glass. (This will also work on windshields but you've got to have enough spit).

Once you get ready to snorkel, spit into your mask, use your fingers to coat the glass completely, then rinse slightly. From then on, if your mask fogs up and you know you were a good spitter, the only reason could be you are exhaling through your nose (which releases moisture and causes fog).

Exhaling through your nose causes leaks and fog. It is easy to do this even though you swear you aren't, because it's an unconscious part of breathing. To catch yourself in the act, hold your nose through the mask; once you catch yourself, it only takes a little bit of concentration to stop using your nose.

The snorkel mouthpiece swivels. This is because you need to have one end in your mouth and the other end sticking out of the water. If your snorkel is not sticking out of the water, this is a very tough sport. To get it in the right position, slide the snorkel along the strap, in front of your ear (right or left side, it doesn't matter unless you are a scuba diver), then bend over and position yourself as if you were snorkeling. Hold the snorkel so it is sticking up, then swivel the mouthpiece to meet your mouth. Now it will stay in the right place. The whole mouthpiece goes in your mouth and your teeth hang onto those little doodads. Believe it or not, it will feel more comfortable in a while. The only thing that is keeping the water from coming into the snorkel around your mouth is the seal of your lips to the tube. The more you look like a chimpanzee, the better, and if you laugh and smile, you leak.

At some point, you are bound to get water in your mask. To get it out, stop in the water and look up slightly, then tip the bottom of the mask away from your face for a few seconds, put the mask back, push the mask against your face to get a good seal and that's it. You don't need to take your mask off and you don't need to tip the mask up forever in order to get the last drop out (it never does come out, there's always one drop left – Murphy's law of snorkeling). If you ever feel a few drops oozing in, push the mask against your face to regain the seal.

To get water out of your snorkel, there are two methods. Method number one is take the snorkel out of your mouth and shake the water out. This method works fine, but the professional method allows you to keep your head in the water and your eyes on the fish. To do this, you use the air in your lungs to push the water out of the snorkel. The easiest way to practice this is: while you are being an excellent chimpanzee, say the word "TWO" with a lot of force. The water will shoot out, impressing yourself and your friends and maybe calling a whale. After your "TWO," don't make your next breath a huge gasp, because if you missed a few drops of water, a big breath will bring those drops in with the air. A normal breath will let them just sit there, and then you can do another TWO or just let them be. The whole time you are snorkeling, you should be breathing normally, except through your mouth not your nose. There is no need to hold your breath (unless you are diving down), or hyperventilate or breathe shallowly.

Fins make you go fast and are good for swimming against currents. You shouldn't be learning to snorkel anywhere there is a current; if you go fast you won't see anything, and fins just complicate the learning process. They really aren't necessary. Seeing and breathing are a whole lot more important. Once you get good at that, then try fins.

If you are using fins, kick with your whole leg in a slow flutter kick, keeping the fins underwater. If you are kicking above the water, you are going nowhere, getting tired fast, plus scaring all the fish away. Remember your feet are at least a foot longer than usual and pay attention to where they are: don't kick off your buddy's mask and don't kick the coral. All the other people on the beach are highly amused by watching someone put their fins on, duck-walk down the beach, then fall through the surf. There is a dignified way to do this: take your fins out into chest-deep water, put on your mask and snorkel so you can see and breath, then bend over and slip the fins on like shoes.

Back to the important stuff – how to put all of this into practice. Check that your mask fits, do your spitting, get the strap up high, position your snorkel, then go out into chest-deep water. Now, bend over and look at your toes. Just look at your toes until you are bored out of your mind. The goal in snorkeling is total boredom: the excitement is what you are going to see, not the gear you are using to see it with. Once you are totally relaxed, let your feet float up, don't do anything, just relax. This is your rest position. You should be able to float like this for hours without moving a muscle. Once you are comfortable, go somewhere, like along the beach, to see which stroke works best. Anything that gets you back from wherever you went, counts – the crawl, the breaststroke, dogpaddle, whatever. Now, double-check that you know how to get water out of your mask and out of your snorkel, then head for the reef.

If you have trouble or are uncomfortable, the first thing you should do (or your buddy should help you do if you are not thinking clearly) is pull your mask off, down around your neck. As soon as you have your eyes and nose back to normal, you will probably feel better. Then turn over and float on your back and relax. If you still feel uncomfortable, you and your buddy should work your way back to shore.

Take your time and practice in the shallow water until you feel comfortable. Almost all the snorkeling accidents happen to people who rush right out to the deep water before they know how to clear their mask and snorkel, or people who overestimate their physical fitness – or people who sit, stand, touch, or brush up against the coral.

## BEACH PICK LIST

If you want to go to the beach, you're definitely on the right island. St. John has 39 accessible beaches, and each offers something different. Some of our best beaches have full facilities: bathrooms, snack bar, showers, and snorkel rentals – while others have no man-made structures at all. Some beaches have lots of people, while others are deserted. There are beautiful long sandy beaches, tiny beaches, and even rocky beaches. We have beaches that can only be reached by hiking and we have beaches which are right on the road. We have beaches which offer excellent snorkeling, others which have great beachcombing. Which one is right for you?

The North Shore of St. John is a whole chain of beautiful white sandy beaches. Some of these beaches can be walked to from Cruz Bay, while most of the rest can be reached by taxi. These are the beaches to go to first.

Once you've had your fill of the North Shore, then the Salt Pond and Lameshur Roads, East End Road, and South Shore Roads can be explored. Most of these beaches require a rental car/jeep to get to and most of them are not huge, wide, sandy beaches, but are well worth visiting if you have the time and wheels.

Nudity is illegal under Virgin Islands law. It is also against National Park Policy. If you are caught, you might be ticketed or arrested or ignored. By identifying the few unofficial nude beaches, I am not encouraging you to strip but rather forewarning those of you who might be offended.

The Virgin Islands has a 'free beach' law (Chapter 10. Open Shorelines. Section 401 to 403) which allows the public to use any beach or shoreline area within 50 feet of the low tide line. However, this law does not allow people to trespass on or across private property. Thus, a few beaches which are totally surrounded by private property and have no traditional access – can only be accessed via water. I repeat: there is no such thing as a private beach in the VI. However, some beaches can only be accessed by boat or by swimming.

Here is a "pick list" of the beaches located on each road, with detailed descriptions of each beach on the following pages.

### NORTH SHORE ROAD BEACHES

Most of St. John's classic, tropical, white sand, palm-tree-lined beaches are on the North Shore. The beaches, in order from closest to Cruz Bay are: Salomon, Honeymoon, Caneel Bay, Hawksnest, Gibney's, Jumbie, Trunk Bay, Peter Bay, Cinnamon Bay, Maho, Little Maho, Francis and Waterlemon.

### HOW TO GET THERE

Salomon and Honeymoon can only be reached by hiking from Cruz Bay or from Caneel Resort. Little Maho Bay requires a short steep hike to reach from the road. Peter Bay Beach can only be reached via water. Waterlemon is about a mile down a dirt road that is no longer passable to cars – you have to hike. All the rest are just a few minutes' walk from the North Shore Road.

Our local taxis will be happy to take you to any of these beaches as far as Cinnamon Bay. From Cinnamon onwards however, a taxi *might* take you. If you find one that says yes, be sure to make arrangements for it to come back and pick you up. (Of course, the Maho Shuttle will also take you right to the campground to get to Little Maho Beach.).

MOST FACILITIES: Trunk Bay, Cinnamon Bay, Little Maho Bay

CAN WALK TO FROM CRUZ BAY: Salomon Beach, Honeymoon Beach, Caneel Bay

CLOSEST BY CAR/TAXI TO CRUZ BAY: Hawksnest Beach

CAN REACH BY TAXI: Caneel Bay Beach, Hawksnest Beach, Gibney's Beach, Jumbie Beach, Trunk Bay Beach, Cinnamon Bay Beach, Maho Beach, Francis Bay Beach

SHORT STEEP HIKE TO REACH FROM ROAD: Little Maho

LONG HIKE REQUIRED FROM ROAD: Waterlemon

WIDE, LONG SANDY BEACHES: Caneel Bay, Hawksnest, Trunk Bay, Cinnamon Bay, Maho Bay, Francis Bay

SMALL SANDY BEACHES: Salomon, Honeymoon, Gibney's, Jumbie, Peter Bay, Little Maho, Waterlemon

LOTS OF PEOPLE: Trunk Bay, Cinnamon Bay, Little Maho, Caneel Bay

REEFS TO SNORKEL: Salomon, Hawksnest, Gibney's, Jumbie, Trunk Bay, Peter Bay, Cinnamon Bay, Little Maho, Waterlemon

CAYS (small islands) TO SNORKEL: Trunk Bay, Cinnamon Bay, Waterlemon

BEST SNORKELING: Trunk Bay, Jumbie, Waterlemon

NUDISTS: Salomon, Jumbie. (Being nude is illegal under VI law.)

SHALLOW WATER A LONG WAY OUT (great for small kids): Maho Bay

ON THE BUS ROUTE: none

## SALT POND AND LAMESHUR ROAD BEACHES

Salt Pond Road is on the "other side" of St. John and has some beautiful white sand beaches, just like the North Shore Road, but also offers some other styles of beach design. The beaches reached by this road, in order from Coral Bay are: Johnson Bay, Friis Bay, Drunk Bay, Salt Pond Beach, Ram Head Trail Beach, Great Lameshur, Little Lameshur, Europa Bay and Reef Bay.

Since these beaches are on the east and south shores, they are protected from the Northern Swells (St. John's version of a blizzard). So if you can't snorkel the North Shore because of northern swells, it will be calm at Salt Pond and Lameshur.

HOW TO GET THERE: The bus runs as far as Salt Pond. Taxis do not normally go to Coral Bay or Salt Pond, and they never go on the Lameshur Road. Check with your hotel or campground's activities desk to see if there is a Salt Pond Trip. Otherwise, you are going to need a rental jeep to go to any of these beaches. The terrible hill on the road to Lameshur Bay is now paved, but you may still need four-wheel drive and many rental companies prefer that you don't take their cars to Lameshur. It is possible to walk the last part of the road to the beach (about 1 mile over a hot, steep hill).

It takes about 1 hour to get from Cruz Bay to Salt Pond, so it's possible to do this trip in half a day. However, there is so much to do at Salt Pond and Lameshur that it's better to make a full day of it, maybe even stopping for dinner at one of the restaurants in Coral Bay on the way back.

MOST FACILITIES: Little Lameshur, Salt Pond Bay

SHORT HIKE REQUIRED FROM ROAD: Salt Pond Bay

LONG HIKE REQUIRED FROM ROAD: Drunk Bay, Ram Head Trail Beach, Europa Bay, Reef Bay

LONG, WIDE SANDY BEACHES: Salt Pond Bay, Little Lameshur, Reef Bay

ROCKY BEACHES: Johnson Bay, Drunk Bay, Ram Head Trail Beach, Great Lameshur, Europa Bay

DIFFICULT SWIMMING, GREAT BEACHCOMBING: Drunk Bay

LOTS OF PEOPLE: none (now that Concordia is larger, there are more people at Little Lameshur and Salt Pond Bay but it still can't be considered crowded)

REEFS TO SNORKEL: all except Drunk Bay

BEST SNORKELING: Salt Pond Bay

NUDISTS: None

DIFFICULT ROAD TO REACH: Great Lameshur, Little Lameshur, Europa, Reef Bay.

ON THE BUS ROUTE: Johnson, Friis, Drunk, Salt Pond

## EAST END ROAD BEACHES

The East End Road is also on the "other side" of the island. There are no huge sandy National Park beaches out here, just beautiful little beaches tucked into small bays and coves where you might want to try snorkeling. There is also a very nice mangrove swamp snorkeling spot. The beaches in order from Coral Bay are: Brown Bay, Princess Bay, Haulover North, Haulover South, Hansen Bay, Long Bay, Privateer Bay.

HOW TO GET THERE: Rental car/jeep is the only way. The bus does not go to the East End, taxis will not go, and hitchhiking is very difficult because there is so little traffic on this road. The road to Privateer Bay requires four-wheel drive (4WD) capacity. Hiking is the only way to get to Brown Bay.

MOST FACILITIES: none

SHORT HIKE REQUIRED FROM ROAD: Haulover North

LONG HIKE REQUIRED FROM ROAD: Brown Bay

SMALL SANDY BEACHES: Hansen Bay, Brown Bay

ROCKY BEACHES: Privateer Bay, Haulover South, Haulover North, Long Bay

LOTS OF PEOPLE: none

REEFS TO SNORKEL: Hansen Bay, Long Bay, Brown Bay, Privateer Bay, Haulover North, Haulover South

MANGROVE SNORKELING: Princess Bay

SEAGRASS SNORKELING: Brown Bay

BEST SNORKELING: Hansen Bay, Long Bay, Brown Bay

NUDISTS: none

DIFFICULT ROAD TO REACH: Privateer Bay

ON THE BUS ROUTE: none

## SOUTH SHORE BEACHES
The South Shore Beaches are found in Cruz Bay, along the South Shore Road and along the Fish Bay Road. The National Park does not own this stretch; it is the developed side of St. John. The beaches, in order from Cruz Bay are: Cruz Bay Beach, Frank Bay, Turner Bay, Great Cruz Bay, Chocolate Hole, Hart Bay, Monte Bay, Klein Bay, Dittlif-Rendezvous side, Dittlif-Fish Bay side, and Parret Bay.

HOW TO GET THERE: Cruz Bay Beach, Frank Bay, and Turner Bay are all within easy walking distance from Cruz Bay. Taxis will take you to the Westin Hotel, which is on Great Cruz Bay Beach. If you have a large group or are lucky, a taxi might take you to Chocolate Hole Beach or to the trail for Hart Bay Beach. For Monte Bay Beach, Klein Bay Beach, both Dittlif Beaches and Parret Bay Beach you will need a rental jeep or can try hitchhiking. Almost all of the South Shore Beaches are not on the main road; they are down small roads or require a short hike.

MOST FACILITIES: Great Cruz Bay

SHORT HIKE REQUIRED FROM ROAD: Hart Bay, Monte Bay, Dittlif-Rendezvous side, Dittlif-Fish Bay side.

DIFFICULT HIKE REQUIRED FROM ROAD: Parret Bay

SANDY BEACHES: Cruz Bay, Great Cruz Bay, Chocolate Hole, Parret Bay

NOT FOR SWIMMING: Turner Bay (barge traffic)

LOTS OF PEOPLE: Great Cruz Bay, Cruz Bay

REEFS TO SNORKEL: Cruz Bay, Frank Bay, Hart Bay, Klein Bay, Dittlif-Fish Bay Side, Parret Bay.

DIFFICULT SNORKELING: Hart Bay (big waves), Great Cruz Bay (poor visibility), Cruz Bay (too many boats), Frank Bay (difficult entry into water), Dittlif-Fish Bay side (big waves, sharks), Parret Bay (big waves).

SEAGRASS SNORKELING: Chocolate Hole

BEST SNORKELING: Frank Bay

NUDISTS: none

DIFFICULT ROAD TO REACH: Parret Bay

ON THE BUS ROUTE: none

## BEACHES IN DETAIL

# NORTH SHORE ROAD BEACHES

### SALOMON BEACH AND HONEYMOON BEACH

These two small white sand beaches, with palm trees providing plenty of shade, can only be reached by hiking the Lind Point Trail, either from Cruz Bay or from Caneel Bay Resort. There are no facilities at either beach (please check update chapter for additional Honeymoon info).

Salomon Beach is a pretty beach with snorkeling on the reef to the left, or the very nice reef between it and Honeymoon Beach to the right. Not very many people come here since it requires hiking. Its seclusion has made it our unofficial nudist beach, so if that would offend you, it would be better to pick another beach to visit. (It is against both Park policy and VI law to go nude on any beach.) Just a little further on the trail is Honeymoon Beach, another white sand beach that attracts few people (but they usually keep their bathing suits on here). The serenity of Honeymoon is disrupted when the day trip boats arrive from St. Thomas and disgorge a large mass of tourists, but they usually only stay for a hour or so.

Honeymoon used to be the home of a large number of stingrays that became so spoiled by people feeding them that they made swimming there almost impossible. Just one foot in the water was enough to bring the whole mob boiling towards you, looking for handout. These stingrays were definitely not good at taking 'no' for an answer! They'd hang around you hoping for food until someone else got in the water, then this aggressive mob of underwater beggars would go harass the newcomer. Hurricane Hugo dispersed the gang, and they (thankfully) haven't regrouped.

The Lind Point Trail – which is a nice, not too steep, very well-maintained trail – starts behind the National Park Headquarters in Cruz Bay. It first takes you to Salomon Beach (.9 miles), next Honeymoon Beach (1.0 miles), then Caneel Bay Beach and the resort. Most people hike from Cruz Bay to the beaches then return the same way, but an alternative is to walk to Salomon, continue to Honeymoon Beach, then go on to Caneel where you can catch a taxi back to Cruz Bay. Another possibility is to hike back on the Margaret Hill Trail.

### CANEEL BAY BEACH

Caneel Bay Beach is one of seven beaches in the Caneel Bay Resort. Visitors are welcome, but there are a few rules: you can go to the restaurants, the gift shop (which has cold drinks), use the bathrooms, walk around the plantation ruins, and hike the National Park's Turtle Point Trail. During high season someone at the visitor parking lot will probably ask you to sign in as a day guest – go ahead, it doesn't cost anything. If you are arriving from the Lind Point Trail, don't worry about signing in. The beach that Caneel encourages visitors to go to is Caneel Bay

Beach, right in front of the registration building. The white sand beach always has people on it and has a floating platform a bit offshore that's fun to dive off. The chairs are reserved for guests only, as are the water toys (windsurfers, sunfish, and kayaks). The best snorkeling is over by the point to the right, but occasionally there are turtles right in front of the beach. A little way past the buildings on the left is the outflow pipe from the reverse osmosis plant. This pipe discharges water that is very salty and a little warm, which attracts eels and other critters. (Please check Update Chapter for more Caneel info)

## HAWKSNEST BEACH

Hawksnest Beach features the closest reef to the shore – it comes right up to the sand and is a very popular beach because it's the first one you get to driving from town. There are covered picnic areas with barbecue pits, so lots of local parties are held here. The other facilities are changing rooms and fancy latrines.

The sandy beach changes shape with each passing storm and has only a few places under the sea grape trees where you can find shade. Usually this area is already occupied by the constant crowd (by St. John standards) of people and kids. If you are trying to find other kids for your child to play with, this is the place to go after school hours.

The snorkeling is easy but the fish and reefs are not as spectacular as elsewhere. Don't forget to pay attention to how close your belly is to the reef, as the water here gets pretty shallow in spots. A young stingray patrols the shallow water along the entire length of the beach, but don't worry – he is so amazingly good at dodging snorkelers that he's never been stepped on.

You can't (easily) climb over the rocks to get to the other beach to the right (Gibney's Beach) but you can swim there or go by road. The small sandy beach to the left can only reached by swimming – you'll probably be the only one on it. The reef just off this beach has great holes and mini-caves full of shy fish. Marathon swimmers could make it over to the Caneel Resort beach way to the left. (If you are not sure you are a marathon swimmer, then you're not.)

There are baby bay rum trees planted in the grass around the parking lot, and donkeys arrive daily to scavenge the garbage cans. About three days after the full moon, Hawksnest is host to some little critters called Glow Worms. These are ½ - inch long worms in the sea that come close to shore once a month to mate. They flash like fireflies – the male flashes at one rate, the female at another. If you wade in the water shining a flashlight, the little glow worms will come to see what sex you are. You can carefully scoop them up in a cup (or a mayonnaise jar for you traditionalists) to check them out. Please return them to the sea afterwards.

## GIBNEY'S BEACH

From the small parking area on the North Shore Road, a dirt road leads to Gibney's Beach (or Little Hawksnest or Oppenheimer's Beach) part of which is a National Park beach and part of which is not (this gets complicated, hang in there). The Gibneys sold a small portion of their land to Mr. Robert Oppenheimer (the inventor of the atom bomb). His daughter (who committed suicide by hanging herself) left it to the "Children of St. John" in her will. The Oppenheimer house was renovated by the VI government and is available for use by the community. This is the land and beach with the yellow building. Next-door is John Gibney's private property, where his widow has guesthouses and sometimes runs a beach bar. Past that is the rest of the Gibney family's beach which has been sold to the National Park, but they haven't taken possession of it yet. What this means is you can go anywhere on the beach itself, wander around the yellow building, visit John's bar if it is open, but do not trespass on the land around the large stone house.

There are no facilities at Gibney's Beach, although the yellow building can be used for a changing room or to get out of the rain. Gibney's Beach is sandy, not as wide as Hawksnest, but offers lots of shade. Since it is not completely a National Park beach, people with dogs and horses come here. If you object to pets on the beach, please go to another one. You may have to wade in the water to get from the building to the beach – which is fun and a lot better than walking onto the private property that borders the beach. Snorkeling here is also not spectacular, but the rocks on the right lead over to a hidden cove with a tiny sandy beach, which is excellent for Robinson-Crusoe-type castaway fantasies. A few feet to the left on that beach is a difficult rope trail leading up to the road.

## JUMBIE BEACH

From the three-car parking lot on the North Shore Road, it is a short walk down the trail to Jumbie Beach. *Jumbie* is a West Indian word for ghosts. This beach and the whole Denis Bay Plantation surrounding it is supposed to be haunted because the plantation owner and overseer for the plantation were brutal and killed slaves regularly. One story is that the owner or overseer used to bury slaves up to their necks in the sand then play a game similar to bowling. During the slave revolt, the Europeans from this plantation were reportedly chopped up and stuffed down the well. (This well, is, ahem, no longer in use.) I personally, have never encountered a ghost on this beach.

This small sandy beach is not well-known (although now that the new speed bumps have been built it is a lot easier to spot) and therefore not usually crowded. It is occasionally used by nudists. There are no facilities at Jumbie Beach. The reef starting to the left of the beach offers nice snorkeling; you can follow the reef around the point to the underwater cliffs. Beware of shortcuts – the reef is very shallow in the center of it, and you can get scraped pretty good unless you stick to following the perimeter. To the right of the beach is another reef sticking straight out from the cliff that is also very good for snorkeling.

## TRUNK BAY BEACH

Trunk Bay, located on the North Shore Road, is the showpiece beach of the National Park, and thus hosts a large volume of visitors. There is a $4-per-person admission fee (16 and under are free) that also admits you to the Annaberg Ruins but only if you go on the same day and you don't lose your ticket. The ticket collector is not on duty 24 hours a day so you will not be able to pay the fee after 4:00 pm or before 9:00 am.

The magnificent white sand beach is over a quarter mile long, lined with palm and sea grape trees. Facilities (open from 9:00 to 4:00) include – real bathrooms, a changing room, a gift shop, a snack bar, a public telephone, lifeguards, fresh water showers (water not always available), snorkel rentals (at the gift shop) and small lockers for valuables. There is an underwater trail with signs on the bottom of the ocean telling you what you are looking at. (Occasionally the fish are uncooperative, but generally they do stay next to their appropriate signs.)

Trunk Bay, because of its facilities, is where the tour groups visit, especially cruise ship tour groups. This means that there can be a sudden influx of hundreds of sunburnt snorkelers eagerly thrashing their way around the trail. Generally these groups stay less than 2 hours, so you can wait them out or come early in the day to avoid them.

The reef has taken a beating over the years from so many visitors, but the incredible variety of fish don't seem to mind a steady stream of beginner snorkelers tromping through their living room – they just ignore all the people and go about their fish business.

Start with the snorkel trail – from the white buoy out to the red one, back to the blue one, a big triangle – and then (if you are a decent snorkeler), continue along the left side of the island into all the coves, then go back the same way. The lifeguards don't want you to swim around the island because they lose sight of you, and the back side of the island has a strong current. If you start on the right side and continue around you usually have to swim against this current. This also brings you very close to the boat traffic lane. The Tortola ferry captains might not see you in the water.

The right side of the island is rocky and has far fewer fish than the coral side – except when the Tarpon have herded a large school of fry against the island.

A nice loop is to walk to the very far right end of the beach, then snorkel out to where there is a small reef. Frequently you will meet a large, 4-foot barracuda named **Charlie** in this area. Afterwards you can swim over to the island and snorkel back along it to the beach. The far left end of the beach also has reefs – they jut straight out from the cliffs. During high season the National Park rangers give a guided snorkel tour once a week at Trunk Bay.

Trunk Bay got its name from either a corruption of the Danish word for Leatherback turtle, or for the neat little triangular-shaped, hard-bodied fish called Trunk fish, take your pick. After the plantation days, a guest inn was built in Trunk Bay, managed by the Boulon family.

In 1958 Mr. Rockefeller bought it and turned it over to the Park. There were a number of small houses up the hill (on the right end of the beach) that the Park tore down. They left the one that is being used as government housing for the Chief Ranger.

The food at the snack bar is not bad. They also have beer, juice, soda, and bottled water (no coffee). Every since the National Park evicted the feral cats, there has been a major Alfred-Hitchcock-type problem with seagulls and thrushies stealing your French fries. The gift shop has a good fish-identification waterproof card as well as the normal selection of T-shirts and souvenirs, film, cigarettes, lighters, hats, suntan lotion, etc. They will rent out masks, fins, snorkels (some security deposit required), flotation belts, and beach chairs. In the parking lot, over by the sign saying 'Taxi Drop Off Zone,' is a large clump of giant bamboo. Across the road are some ruins from the Trunk Plantation days, which are (according to Park officials) unsafe to wander through.

## PETER BAY BEACH
Peter Bay Beach is part of an exclusive and expensive subdivision. As you can see by looking up at the hillside, the architectural goal of the millionaire owners appears to be "cover every square inch of the lot with a building."

Peter Bay has a small white sand beach with plenty of shade from the coconut palms and sea grape trees. This area used to have excellent snorkeling, but now the reef is dying and looks terrible (maybe all that development?). So that fact – that the surrounding the beach is all private property and access by the public is only via the water – is no longer such a great loss. Unless a property owner invites you in, you have to swim from Cinnamon Bay or use a boat.

The swim from Cinnamon is a moderately lengthy one, but there are numerous stopping places. The rope hammocks attached to the palm trees along the sandy beach are private. The houses built along the beach are also private, so please respect their privacy.

The reef continues all the way around the point. It is possible to keep going and end up in Trunk Bay if you are a long-distance swimmer.

## CINNAMON BAY BEACH
Cinnamon Bay Beach is a part of the Cinnamon Bay Campground, which is located on the North Shore Road. It is a huge, wide beach with a little island offshore, similar to Trunk Bay. It has all the things that people coming for a week's stay in Paradise might need – bathrooms, showers, a small grocery store, public telephones, a buffet-style restaurant which opens three times a day, a gift shop, snorkel gear rentals, a small museum, windsurfing and sea kayak rentals, and even Sunday volleyball games.

Cinnamon Bay is also the site of a very successful **archeology dig** that has uncovered a tremendous amount of artifacts from a Taino Indian village, leading to a great deal of brand new information on the Tainos, and on St. John. Whenever funds can be found, there will be a museum constructed on St. John to house the artifacts and document the findings. Volunteer diggers are frequently needed, contact **Ken Wild** at 693-5230.

The beach is reached from the entrance drive by walking straight down the gravel road until you get to the gift shop (you pass one of the bath houses along the way). Don't be disappointed; this is not the main beach. If you turn to the right, walk past the archeology dig and follow the beach around the trees, you'll find the long, wide, sandy beach. The area in front of the gift shop and to the left of it is normally used by surfers, windsurfers, and dinghies – that's why it is not marked off with the white buoys that keep boats out.

When the northern swells are running, this is a place where waves really kick up. Even if you think the swells are small, you should respect them. They've come a long way and can pack a considerable wallop. When the waves are not running (which is most of the time), you can snorkel out to the island – but please don't overestimate your swimming ability. It's a bit of a swim to get to the island and back, and there are no lifeguards here. The coral isn't great until you get all the way out to the island; the back side is especially good.

Other possible snorkeling destinations are to the right around America Point (this will eventually take you into Francis Bay and to Maho Beach, but it's a long swim) or to the left over to Little Cinnamon Beach and then to Peter Bay Beach.

There is an easy-to-find trail that scrambles over the hill to Little Cinnamon Beach – a narrow sandy beach that can disappear when the surf is up. The remains of a stone building are in the bushes off to the left. To find the airplane wreck (possibly a Piper Cub), enter the water at the beginning of the beach where the reef and rocks stop, then swim straight out about 20 yards (the water will be about 15 feet deep). Notice how amazingly clean the propeller and wing are – after 40 years underwater – no coral, barnacles, algae or rust. If boat builders used the same material, no one would need bottom paint!

## MAHO BAY BEACH

Maho Bay Beach is the closest beach to the road on St. John. It is so close that during storms, the sea comes right over the North Shore Road. The best part of the beach is at the far end to the right.

In order to get there, you first have to pass a long building fronted by a stone wall with a few parking places alongside. This community building used to be available for public use but now is just a falling-down ruin. Various groups have rehabilitated this building after storms, but the sea continues to win the battle. Hopefully someone will come rescue it again.

The dilapidated trailer that sat next door to this building for years finally was completely demolished by a hurricane. The trailer and the cute little house surrounded by flowers on the right side of the road belong to two sisters (one sister recently died, the other, Erma, is in a nursing home) who have a serious, long-term disagreement with the VI National Park. For many years they have been battling the park over who owns which part of Maho Beach. Recently the Trust for Public Land succeeded in reaching an agreement with all the owners of the beach and hillside so most of this land will be undeveloped.

Most people are surprised to learn that the National Park does not own all the land on the North Shore. This may be because the area shaded on the official Park map is not showing Park-owned land, but where the Park could extend to if they bought the land. Confusing, right?

Of course, most of the 'continental' visitors to St. John think very highly of Mr.

Rockefeller for buying up a portion of the island and donating it to the National Park - but some native Virgin Islanders do not.

They remember that Mr. Rockefeller's first 'plan' for St. John included acquiring the remaining private land through condemnation and moving all the displaced people to Fish Bay. This bill was approved by the Assistant Secretary of the Interior and passed by the US Senate, before St. Johnians like Theovald 'Mooie' Moorehead heard about it at the last minute and stopped him.

Unfortunately, even today, there are still a couple of local families in court battles over boundary disputes with the Park. I personally think that as long as the Park produces maps implying that my house is on their property, they should either help pay my property tax bill, or change the map.

Maho Beach is extremely well-protected, and even when all the other beaches on the North Shore are getting pounded with waves, this beach is calm. The water is very shallow for a long way out. This makes it popular for non-swimmers and families with small kids. Parking can be a problem. You might have to go around the corner to park off the side of the road or go park up near the community building. The snorkeling here is different – the sea grass and the sandy bottom attract turtles, especially easy to see in the early morning and just before sunset feeding times. Of course no-see-ums and mosquitoes also feed at sunset (on you!), so stay in the water. The rocks to the right offer some good snorkeling. There are always some nice fish, and occasionally tarpon can be seen. Continue swimming around the point and you'll come to Little Maho, the Maho Bay Campground beach.

I think you have to be truly dedicated and/or a little crazy to consider running and biking up St. John hills in tropical heat a fun thing to do, but there is a surprisingly large group of triathletes who use Maho as a training ground for all three sports – swimming, biking, and running.

The Goat Trail to Maho Campground starts right where the road turns away from the beach. It parallels the beach, and then heads up the hill to end up at the campground front desk.

## FRANCIS BAY BEACH

Francis Bay Beach is a long, wide sandy beach with very few people, except when the Caneel Resort boat comes in for a picnic lunch. The beach is down a dirt road off the main road leading to Maho Bay Campground. It can also be reached by hiking the Francis Bay Trail (an excellent birdwatching nature trail). The Maho Bay Campground taxi will drop you off at the trail or the dirt road.

Francis Beach offers picnic tables, fancy latrines, and barbeque pits for facilities. The bottom is mostly sandy. There is a small reef area well along Mary's Point (that's past the right end of the beach) and another little reef between Francis and Little Maho to the left. When large schools of bait fish (fry) come to visit, there are usually some tarpon escorting them. Francis is very well protected from waves and has a long stretch of nice sandy beach. However, it has a lot of bugs after it rains and/or at dusk. It is a great beach for taking a nap – just beware of sunburn.

## LITTLE MAHO BEACH

Little Maho Beach is part of Maho Bay Campground. They welcome visitors, but request that you help them conserve water (this means you can't use the showers) and respect the privacy of the guests (don't go snooping around the tents). The beach is a small sandy one, usually with lots of people. It takes about 10 minutes to get to the beach from the parking lot. It is also possible to swim over from Francis Bay or Maho Beach. The campground has a restaurant and bar (only open at meal times), bathrooms, a small general store, public pay phones, snorkel and beach toy rentals. The Campground has its own taxi shuttle service from Cruz Bay at scheduled times all day and even some at night.

From the Campground parking lot, follow the boardwalk and stairs downward past the store and front desk. Then it's another 180 stairs down to the Little Maho beach. At the bottom, you'll find a nice little sandy beach with lots of trees, sea kayak, windsurfer, sunfish, and snorkel rentals. If there is a volleyball game or any other activity going on, it is easy to join in. The best snorkeling is over to the left; there are rocks and some coral all the way around the point to Big Maho Beach. Snorkeling to the right goes by some rocks and over to Francis Beach. (Please check the Update chapter for more information about Maho Campground.)

## WATERLEMON BEACH

Waterlemon Beach (no, not watermelon, water<u>lemon</u>) is a tiny sandy and rocky beach that is not very impressive – but the nearby snorkeling is superb, especially out around the little offshore cay. There are no facilities. (This beach is technically named Leinster Bay Beach, but Leinster Bay is very large and no one understands exactly where I'm talking about if I use that name, so I'm going to keep calling it Waterlemon). The beach is reached by going a mile down the Leinster Bay Trail from the paved road at Annaberg Ruins (which is about a half mile from the North Shore Road). This trail used to be a very bad dirt road but various storms have washed it out – it is 100% impossible to drive to Waterlemon beach. However, if you are incredibly pigheaded, and willing to tear the bottom out of your rental car, you can drive a few minutes down this road before it becomes impassable. If you are one of the first ones there will be a place to park, if not you will have to BACK UP all the way back to the pavement because there is nowhere to turn around. It is much easier (and smarter) to park in the Annaberg parking lot and walk. The Maho Bay Campground shuttle will now drop you off at the parking lot.

Follow the former road along the shoreline. There is nice snorkeling along this stretch and the water birds are very active here. After about 15 minutes you will reach a small beach. Snorkeling is great in every direction. Along the shoreline to the right there are lots of fish. This area is patrolled by baby barracuda keeping their exact territorial boundaries clearly identified – each one owns about 20 feet. (Once these babies grow up, they leave the area).

The very best snorkeling is out around that little island. It's called Waterlemon Cay. You have to be a decent swimmer in reasonable condition (no lifeguards here) to get there. Don't chance it if you're doubtful of your abilities.

In order to swim the shortest distance to Waterlemon Cay you can follow the little shoreline trail that leads you around to the take-off point.

Sometimes there's a bit of current running, keep that in mind for the swim back. The reef almost encircles the cay with incredible soft and hard coral on the back side, so it's well worth going around the whole tiny island (usually it is best to swim counterclockwise around, but if the currents are running go the other way). I like to sunbathe and rest awhile on the little beach on the cay before I swim back. Just in front of the beach is a good place for seeing large starfish – they are either here having an enormous starfish party or they are completely gone, I haven't found anyone that one can explain why or what the schedule is.

# SALT POND AND LAMESHUR ROAD BEACHES

### JOHNSON BAY

Johnson Bay is a large bay with multiple small beaches. Two of them are right alongside Salt Pond Road – one very rocky but the other has a bit of sand. They are not the prettiest swimming or snorkeling spots, but there is an extensive reef by the rocky point, and way, way out there is the reef that protects the bay from the open ocean.

The first beach is located right in front of the **Shipwreck Restaurant.** It has a bathroom as well as food and drink. The second beach is a few minutes walk over the hill and further down the road in front of what used to be a Grocery Store. Even further down the road across from the monstrous Calabash Boom housing project, is a large chunk of shoreline that was purchased by someone who decided he needed to erect a chain-link fence, which closed off one of the traditional access to the beach. But at the far end of that stretch is an entrance that he doesn't own. The sign says it is a private road that you are not supposed to drive your car down. Walking on the road is OK though.

### FRIIS BAY BEACH

The Friis Bay beach is located just off the Salt Pond Road, right in front of **Miss Lucy's Restaurant.** It is a small sandy beach, with some reefs out there to the left. On Sundays this is a great place for brunch, with live music – anyone not interested in eating can go for a snorkel.

### SALT POND BAY BEACH

Salt Pond Beach is long and wide, has plenty of clean white sand, and is great for snorkeling. The trail leading to Salt Pond Beach is a 5-minute walk from the parking lot. Facilities are a few picnic tables and a deluxe outhouse. There are very few trees for shade. Now that Concordia Resort is expanding, this beach has a lot more visitors.

The gorgeous crystal-clear water in the bay is excellent for snorkeling. There are plenty of fish. The right side is rocky with some coral; the left has big clusters of reef and rocks. In the middle of the bay is sea grass – perfect for turtles, conch, and stingrays. I have seen turtles, moray eels, octopuses, stingrays, angel fish, squid, lobsters, and tons of little colorful fish here all in one afternoon. If you are a good enough swimmer, the almost-submerged rocks out in the bay are also an excellent place to snorkel. They have some of the best coral to be seen on St. John, plus lots of beautiful fish.

### DRUNK BAY BEACH

Drunk Bay Beach is rocky and pounded by waves. It is NOT good for swimming or snorkeling, but it is excellent for beachcombing. There are no facilities. To get there, take the Drunk Bay Trail from Salt Pond Beach. It's about a 10-minute walk. Drunk Bay is not the place where St. Johnians go to party. Numerous shipwrecks and drownings have taken place here. Its name is a corruption of the word *drunken,* meaning 'drowned' in Dutch Creole. The coastline here is wild, rugged, and foreboding. Drunk Bay does not have a protecting reef, like so many St. John bays. It's open sea, and there is nothing to slow down the waves that roll in all the way from Africa. What a contrast to the other, more tranquil St. John beaches!

The ceaseless waves here bring in all kinds of interesting debris like driftwood, pieces of wrecked boats, garbage, and shoes (never both of the pair though). Since the Virgin Islands is in the middle of the drug-smuggling runs to Florida, sometimes "square fish or burlap seafood or square grouper" wash ashore here; if you find one you are supposed to contact the authorities. (Generally speaking, our jails are not nice places.) The Environmental Protection Agency is also paying large rewards to anyone providing enough evidence to successfully prosecute cruise ships for illegal garbage-dumping.

Some very creative people have started what has become a tradition – using pieces of coral and debris to make large (4 feet and up) people and animal "pictures" on the rocks. Scramble up to the top of the cliff to really appreciate the artwork, and add your own creation.

## RAM HEAD TRAIL BEACH
The Ram Head Trail Beach is rocky and requires hiking about 15 minutes from Salt Pond Beach on the Ram Head Trail to get there. There are no facilities.

The Ram Head Trail Beach offers a nice break to cool off on the hike to and from Ram Head. The beach is made of large different-colored stones rounded by the surf – perfect samples of all the different types of local rocks. The small waves pushing the rocks around make a wonderful soothing sound.

The snorkeling here is good, but watch where you put your feet when entering – there are sea urchins in the rocks. The large rocks and cliffs over to the right are good snorkeling if the waves are not crashing too heavily and the visibility is good.

## GREAT LAMESHUR BEACH
Great Lameshur Beach is a long, wide, rocky beach good for swimming, snorkeling, beachcombing, and wandering. There are no facilities. The beach is just off the Lameshur Road (you may 4WD to negotiate). This beach is almost always deserted. Snorkeling here is good. There are lots of fish in the rocks. There is no way to walk along this beach to the dock. You have to go back the way you came because there is a massive mangrove swamp and deep water in between. There are reefs off to the left.

You can hike/scramble along the left-hand shore around the point to another small beach and more snorkeling. A long way past that beach, if you are a great rock scrambler, you will eventually come to a little cove that has nice big boulders to snorkel and underwater cement footings left over from the 1950's Tektite research project. Thanks to the Trail Bandit, the path continues along the ridge and comes out at the top of the very steep hill on the Lameshur Road. This is a difficult hike; take lots of water and some snacks.

## LITTLE LAMESHUR BEACH

The beach at Lameshur (actually it's Little Lameshur Bay) is wide and sandy. There are plenty of trees for shade. There are also picnic tables and a deluxe outhouse building. The beach is easy to find – it comes right up to Lameshur Road (road that may require 4WD to negotiate). Little Lameshur Beach is beautiful and is usually not crowded.

Snorkeling along the shoreline to the left is good, and there is a "secret" rocky beach around the corner. The rocks to the right can be snorkeled as well.

## EUROPA BAY BEACH

Europa Bay Beach is rocky and frequently has waves. There are no facilities. The beach is about a 30-minute hike from the end of the Lameshur Road (a dirt road requiring 4WD to negotiate) on the Lameshur Trail.

Europa Bay has small reefs, but if there are waves, snorkeling and swimming can be difficult. This beach is hardly ever visited, so you can have it all to yourself. At different times, driftwood washes ashore and becomes wedged in the rocks. With a bit of beachcombing and creativity, these branches can become a "flotsam tree" – a work of art that lasts until a storm takes the branch back out to sea.

## REEF BAY BEACH

Reef Bay Beach is sandy, with lots of reefs to snorkel. There is a disgusting outhouse. The beach is reached by hiking the Reef Bay Trail from Centerline Road (90 minutes); by hiking the Lameshur Trail from Lameshur Road (90 minutes) and taking a left onto the Reef Bay Trail; or by hiking/scrambling from Parret Bay Beach using the Little Reef Bay Trail (40 minutes).

The beach is at the end of the Reef Bay Trail. It is great for cooling off before the long climb back up the trail or while waiting for the National Park boat to pick up your tour group. The snorkeling is good on the outside of the reef to the left, or at the rocks to the right, or even straight out to the turtle grass. This bay is very shallow, which makes the water warm.

The beach is flanked by a large mangrove swamp, so it can get pretty buggy. At the far end of the beach on the left, (wade past where the mangrove trees stick out into the water) there is a salt pond. It requires a bit of bushwhacking but the pond has lots of ducks and birds in it. If you wade further down the beach, it becomes easy to see baby sharks in the bay (lemon and black-tip sharks about 12 inches long) because it is so shallow their fins stick out of the water. Sit down on the beach and look hard for those fins, they might even be patrolling right next to the beach. Once these baby sharks get bigger than 12 inches, they leave this bay and go offshore to bigger and better feeding grounds. They have no interest in people as a food source and are very easily scared when you splash in the water.

# EAST END ROAD BEACHES

## BROWN BAY BEACH

Brown Bay Beach is narrow and sandy, and the bay has excellent snorkeling. There are no facilities. The beach can only be reached by hiking the difficult Johnny Horn Trail from Waterlemon Beach (about 90 minutes) or the Brown Bay Trail from East End Road (about 60 minutes). It is also possible to scramble along the coastline from Waterlemon (at least 90 minutes, difficult).

The beach is not spectacular, but the shallow water is thick with turtle grass making it the perfect nursery for hundreds of baby conch. As you can see by the mountain of conch and whelk shells on the beach, the local fisherman know all about this place. Snorkeling here is very different from the reef areas. There are all kinds of new things to see. Try not to step on the sea grass bed when entering the water. First snorkel around the grass area, then check out the reefs on either side of the bay. The reefs on the left are particularly nice. You are probably going to have this beach mostly to yourselves. Enjoy.

To the left of the beach are ruins from the plantation days. Read *Night of the Silent Drums* then come picture these ruins as one of the major headquarters for the slaves during the 1733 rebellion. The stonework on these buildings is magnificent. Notice the use of coral for the corners – coral can be cut cleanly with a saw when wet, but once dry, coral is as strong as stone and impossible to cut.

## PRINCESS BAY

Princess Bay Beach doesn't really have a beach, but it does have access to some unique mangrove snorkeling. There are no facilities. The beach is right on the side of the East End Road.

Mangrove snorkeling sounds horrible, but isn't. If you've never tried it, you're in for a thrill. It is a fascinating underwater world that is completely different from a reef.

The mangroves provide protection for a tremendous variety of baby fish, crabs, and lobsters until they are big enough to survive on the reef. Get up really close, stick your head through the tangle of roots, and look really hard (take your time) to spot all kinds of crabs, shellfish, and other creepy-crawlers.

The mangroves are a smelly/mucky/buggy swamp only where the tide exposes the sea bottom to the air. Since you snorkel in the water-covered part, there is clear visibility and no smell (unless you don't know how to snorkel in shallow water without hitting the bottom and stirring up the silt – it is best not to use fins).

## HAULOVER BAY SOUTH

Haulover Bay South, a subsection of Round Bay, is a small rocky beach with some patches of sand. There are no facilities. The beach is right on the side of the East End Road.

The beach is not spectacular, but it is the closest beach from Coral Bay and the swimming is fine. Snorkeling is good here, since lots of fish, octopuses and eels prefer rocks to reefs. Beware of the large black sea urchins when entering the water. Snorkel the rocks along either shore, then work your way out to the reefs at either point (pay attention to currents at the points). A little way around the left point is a small rock beach that you can rest on before swimming back.

## HAULOVER BAY NORTH

Haulover Bay North is a rocky beach with very good snorkeling if it's not too choppy. There are no facilities. The beach is reached by a short 5-minute trail from East End Road.

The beach offers a great view of Tortola and Drake's Passage. There are lots of reefs and magnificent coral heads off to the left, which provide super snorkeling if it's a calm day. To the right around the little point is a sandy beach. To get there, scramble over the rocks. While doing so, take time to look at these rocks. This area is a geologist's heaven. This beach is usually deserted.

## HANSEN BAY BEACH

The Hansen Bay Beach, while it has some patches of sand, is mostly rocky. It offers superb snorkeling. There are no facilities. The beach is right alongside the East End Road, under a big tree (no longer occupied by the "dead boat" that sat there for many, many years until I decided to use it as a landmark in the last update – it was sold and moved within months). This small beach has numerous urchins hiding in the shallow water, so look before you step. The snorkeling to the left – out to the point and to Pelican Rock – is excellent. This area has a wide variety of hard and soft corals, which form spectacular ravines and crevasses. An unfortunate squall in 2012, caused a sailboat to be wrecked on the reef. The boating community cleaned up everything as best they could, but the very heavy keel was too heavy to lift so it remains. It will be interesting to watch how fast Mother Nature incorporates the wreck into the reef.

## LONG BAY BEACH

Long Bay Beach is also mostly rocky, but it too offers great snorkeling. There are no facilities. The beach is reached by a short walk (2 minutes) down a little path from the turn-around at the end of East End Road. (This beach also suffers from an identity crisis – it too is sometimes called Hansen Bay beach.)

This beach is on the other side of Pelican Rock from Hansen Beach, so snorkel to the right to get to this excellent snorkel spot. Straight out is turtle grass where you might find turtles or conch or (if you're really lucky) garden eels sticking out of the sand. To the left, long stretches of coral ledges make for excellent snorkeling.

## PRIVATEER BAY BEACH

Privateer Bay Beach is a rocky beach with good snorkeling. It is part of the Privateer Estate sub-division. There are no facilities. The beach is a 2-minute walk from the end of the Privateer Estate Road. This road is now paved the entire way but has very steep stretches that require four-wheel drive, especially after it rains. Follow the road without turning until you see a small right hand road just before the chain (this chain prevents access to yet another subdivision that decided to pave paradise and ruin more pristine bays with runoff and silt). It is about a 10-minute walk down that road to the beach.

This long, rocky beach has good beachcombing. (It continues past the rock outcropping to the right.) The waves occasionally make swimming and snorkeling here difficult or impossible. If it's calm, you can check out the reef right off the beach, another reef way out in the middle of the bay, and the rocks and reefs along the left side. There are numerous fish traps in this area, which has depleted the fish population somewhat. However, these can be interesting to dive on. (Do not tamper with the pots, as they are someone's livelihood.)

# SOUTH SHORE BEACHES

### CRUZ BAY BEACH

Cruz Bay Beach is a pretty sandy beach lined with palm trees. However, the bay is full of boats, which makes swimming difficult. There is a nice snorkeling reef off the point to the left; go to the furthermost end of the beach from town and swim out towards the navigation buoy. (Stay in shallow water, well away from the navigational channel. Snorkelers have been struck by outboard-powered dinghies in this area. Bring a dive flag.) The reef goes all the way around the point and over to Gallows Point beach.

### FRANK BAY BEACH

Frank Bay Beach is mostly rocky but there are some sandy spots. There are no facilities, except the art gallery across the street and Patrick's Food Stand up the hill. The beach is on the side of a small road that connects to Genip Street. It's a 15-minute walk from Cruz Bay.

Access to the water is very difficult as the reef comes right up onto the beach and there are urchins hiding in the rocks. Once in the water, however, the snorkeling is very good.

The shoreline to the left is rocky with some coral (be careful if you continue around the point, there is a very powerful current). Also to the left is the large cement block covered with mesh which is the intake for our reverse osmosis plant (follow the pipe out to the end). Lots of fish have made their home around this man-made reef.

Snorkeling straight out from the beach brings you to the turtle grass area. From the right side of the beach are underwater power cables that bring all of St. John's electricity over from St. Thomas. Snorkeling to the right, there are reefs and rocks all the way along the shoreline, past Gallows Point Condos, around the point and into Cruz Bay. The floating dock at Gallows Point is a favorite place for a large (5-foot) barracuda to hide from the sun.

### TURNER BAY BEACH

Turner Bay Beach is all rocks and is not a great place for swimming. There are no facilities. The bumpy, dirt Fish Fry Drive passes right by the beach. It's about a 10-minute walk from Cruz Bay.

Turner Bay used to be at the mouth of Enighed Pond. This is where we used to hold our weekly community fish fry parties not so long ago. In order to build a sorely needed cargo facility, the pond was opened up to the bay and now a steady stream of large barges goes in and out all day making swimming hazardous. Too bad, because there is still very nice coral in spite of all the waves, oil spills, and boat wakes.

### GREAT CRUZ BAY BEACH

The Great Cruz Bay Beach borders the Westin Hotel. The hotel has restaurants, a gift shop and art gallery, a deli, and a bar by the pool that are also open to the public. (The pool and spa next to it are reserved for hotel guests only.) The Westin is located along the South Shore Road, and the beach is about a 3-minute walk from the parking lot.

The sandy beach is not very wide and in high season is packed with hotel guests. The left side of the beach is the dingy parking area for all of the boat owners anchored out in the bay. Great Cruz Bay has poor visibility much of the time and has no reef, so it is not very good for snorkeling.

## CHOCOLATE HOLE BEACH

Chocolate Hole is a narrow sandy beach with good turtle grass snorkeling. There are no facilities. The beach is at the end of Chocolate Hole East road which is about a 5-minute drive from the South Shore Road (keep going straight following the massive construction mess on the right – do not turn onto Bovacaop Point Road)

Chocolate Hole got its name because of the color of the rocks at the entrance to the bay, not because of the color of the water – the bay has blue water and good visibility. The snorkeling here is different: sea grass, rocky areas, conch, large fish, turtles, lobsters, but very little coral reef.

The new-development folks seem to be determined to change this very healthy bay into a dead, cloudy mess just like Great Cruz Bay, because "their quality resort deserves a white sandy beach just like Caneel" – the fact that they did not BUY a white sandy beach seems to be a minor detail. And the lesson that should have been learned when the Great Cruz Bay developers took a crystal-clear bay and permanently ruined it does not seem matter either.

## HART BAY BEACH

Hart Bay Beach is a rocky beach with a reef that offers good snorkeling when it's calm. There are no facilities. The beach is reached by hiking about 10 minutes on a well-maintained trail. From the South Shore Road, take Chocolate Hole East, left onto Tamarind Road, right onto Cactus Road, at the turnaround look for the Hart Bay Trail sign.

Hart Bay is a subsection of Rendezvous Bay. It is exposed to the open sea, so there are almost always waves. The beach is protected by a large reef, so the swimming is always good. The best snorkeling is on the far side of the reef, but this should only be attempted if it is calm.

## MONTE BAY BEACH

Monte Bay Beach is a small rocky beach with no facilities. To get there, turn off the South Shore Road just before the Fish Bay Road turnoff onto a paved road. Follow this road for a few minutes. Take the first left, and then turn left again onto a dirt road (there is actually a sign for Monte Bay Road). Continue to the end of the road, park, and take the wooden stairs down to the small beach. This corner of Rendezvous Bay frequently has bad visibility due to waves. The rocks on either side can be snorkeled.

## KLEIN BAY BEACH

Klein Bay Beach is a small rocky beach. There are no facilities. The beach is reached by a short walk from the end of the paved road through the sub-division. From Fish Bay Road, turn right onto Klein Bay Drive and go straight (don't turn onto Turtle Point Court). At the Belle Mer villa sign, go right to the two parking spots, then follow the path down to the beach.

This is not a busy beach and the swimming is great. For snorkeling, the rocks and coves to the left are the best. You can check out the turtle grass for conch or turtles. Occasionally dolphins and whales visit this bay but these are best seen from one of the vacation rental villas above.

## DITTLIF POINT BEACH - RENDEZVOUS BAY SIDE

Dittlif Point Beach-Rendezvous Bay side is a long, narrow, mostly sandy beach. There are no facilities. The beach is reached by hiking about 10 minutes from Fish Bay Road on the Dittlif Point road. If the road is not blocked, you can drive to the top of the trail leading to the beach.

Dittlif Point is not part of the National Park, so people with dogs like to come here. Occasionally a fisherman will launch his boat from this beach. The bottom is almost all sea grass, which is fine for snorkeling and swimming. The trail continues past the beach and follows along the rock pools out to the point.

There is a reef around this point which has good snorkeling, but it should only be attempted in very calm weather.

## DITTLIF POINT BEACH - FISH BAY SIDE

Dittlif Point Beach-Fish Bay side is a very small rocky beach. There are no facilities. The beach is reached by hiking about 15 minutes from Fish Bay Road on the Dittlif Point Road.

The Fish Bay side beach is reputed to have excellent snorkeling. I don't know this firsthand because Fish Bay is quite a popular nursery for sharks (Nurse and Lemon sharks, mostly, but some black tips too), and I'm too 'chicken' to go snorkeling with a bunch of protective Mamma sharks around. For those of you who are braver than I am, snorkel the reefs and rocks to the right or the left – and report back if you survive. (According to a few adventurers who did report in, the snorkeling was good but they were disappointed because they did not see hundreds of sharks, just one or two).

## PARRET BAY BEACH

This beach's official name is Parret Bay Beach, but very few people know that. I used to call it the Reef Bay Beach on the Fish Bay side, but a historian convinced me that I have an obligation to use the correct name and a perfect opportunity to educate people in this book. Most people call this beach the Fish Bay Beach (even though it's not on Fish Bay) because it's the best beach in the Fish Bay area. There are no facilities. This beach can be reached from the Reef

Bay Trail by hiking/scrambling about 35 minutes on the Little Reef Bay Trail or it takes about 10 minutes of difficult hiking to get here from the Reef Bay Road. This very bad dirt road is about a 10-minute drive from the paved portion of the Fish Bay Road. From the parking area on the Reef Bay Road, look along the edge of the drop-off for the knotted rope, right next to the telephone pole near a shingled house (the owner of this house is a nudist who likes to prove it to people passing by. Just ignore him). Use this rope to descend down the extremely steep hill, and then follow the trail to the beach.

The beach is long, wide, and sandy, perfect for hanging out but not terrific for swimming. There are usually big waves pounding the coral reef, so snorkeling on the outside of the reef can be dangerous. However, that reef protects some of the beach, so it may be calm enough to swim in the small section that is both protected and not too shallow. The rightmost part of the beach is not protected by a reef – the big waves come right up to shore, which makes for good surfing but bad swimming.

To the right is a tramway that provides deluxe beach access to and from that enormous house for Mr. Gross and his guests. I can't imagine how this tram will be kept in working order in this "hostile to machinery" environment, but I hope I get invited for a ride while it is still new and running well.

To the left, at the far end of the beach, you can scramble around the rocky point (difficult but possible except when the surf is rough) to Little Reef Bay Beach. This is another nice sandy beach, but the water is way too shallow (less than 1 foot deep) for swimming except at the far end. The shallows are an excellent place to spot baby sharks with their fins sticking out of the water. Very good snorkeling can be found on the outside of the reef: enter the water where it finally gets deep and swim straight out past the mooring balls. The reef is to the right. Be careful if there are big waves.

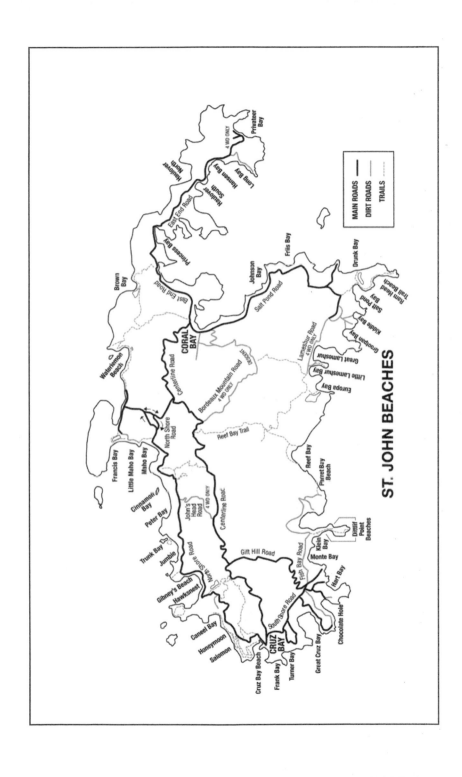

ST. JOHN BEACHES

# THE TRAILS

## HIKING: WANDERING IN PARADISE

St. John is in the tropics. This means it's HOT, HOT, HOT all the time, and you might need to do some things differently while here. While some of our trails gently wind themselves through shady forests, many of our best trails offer almost no shade at all. So be prepared for our tropical-strength sun. It is nearly impossible to overestimate its power.

Use sunscreen, take a wide-brimmed hat, and cover up any skin that's already pink. Rain is not a major problem. Only rarely does it rain all day here. Usually a rainsquall moves in, drenches everything, and withdraws within a few minutes. These rainsqualls can be a nice way to cool off.

The best time for hiking is early in the morning (no bugs and it's cool). Even for good hikers, the heat is going to have an impact. If you are sweating up a storm hiking up a hill, just take a break, sit down and enjoy the view. Isn't that what you came for?

The sun sets early and quickly. St. John has almost exactly 12 hours of sun and 12 of dark. So between 6 and 6:30 pm (in the winter) and 7 and 7:30 pm (in the summer) the sun is going to set – and within minutes – it will be DARK. Don't get unexpectedly caught out at the beach or up a trail.

Have you ever seen the green flash? This rare optical event sometimes occurs as the upper edge of the setting tropical sun appears to be just touching the water on a clear horizon. A brilliant emerald green flash of light is produced for some complicated atmospheric reason. It only lasts a microsecond; you have to be looking for it to observe it. But when it happens, it is quite distinct and startling. (Drinking too many rum Painkillers has also been known to produce the same effect, but that's cheating).

Speaking of drinking reminds me of water – and how much the human body needs fluids here in the tropics. Bring plenty of water with you while hiking. Gatorade, fruit juice and/or water is best, then sodas. Alcoholic beverages are terrible for hiking because they speed up the dehydration process. Being hot and thirsty is miserable – but being dehydrated is dangerous.

Watch where you put your food. Donkeys, mongoose, and thrushie birds are cute but they are also excellent thieves who know what a lunch looks like. Don't leave paper or plastic bags with food in them on the beach or on the trail. Keep your food in something heavier, like a knapsack. It is also a good idea to hang it from a tree high enough that a donkey can't reach it.

There are very few trash barrels along the trails but this does not mean that you can throw your trash away. Please take it back out with you (and pick up anyone else's that you can carry).

Garbage is the only thing you can help yourself to. It is illegal to take any plant or animal or fish or shell or rock or brick or *anything* out of the National Park - everything is protected. Take pictures instead.

There are ruins all over the island and we want to keep them as long as possible. Please don't destroy them by taking pieces out of the walls or by climbing around or thoughtlessly knocking them down.

The reefs are fragile. If you touch or stand on the coral, it dies. Feeding animals is prohibited because it disturbs the natural food chain and often causes aggressive behavior.

At the moment, the National Park has quite a few trail signs up (amazing!). However, the next storm could knock them down and it may take years for them to be replaced. Do not count on signs being there.

Most of the official National Park trails are well-used and easy to follow. Any trails identified as unofficial may not be easy to follow because they are not maintained – pay attention. As with any hike, it is always a good idea to tell someone where you are going. St. John is quite small – if you get lost, head downhill and eventually you will get to the ocean – or head uphill and eventually you'll get to the road (probably Centerline). But getting lost is usually no fun, so stay on the trail. Camping is only permitted in the Cinnamon Bay Campground or at Maho Bay Campground. If the rangers catch you camping elsewhere in the park, you'll be ticketed.

With the increase in development comes an increase in traffic – especially very large construction vehicles. When you are walking on a road, make sure you walk on the **outside of a curve** so you can jump off the pavement when a truck comes speeding around the corner. On the straight stretches, it doesn't really matter whether you walk with the traffic or against it, what matters is which side gives you more room to get out of the way. Walk defensively!

# TRAIL PICK LIST

Hiking one of St. John's trails is a wonderful way to experience the island. Many of the trails lead to secluded beaches. The detailed information for each trail is organized by the length of hiking time required.

LESS THAN 15 MINUTES ONE WAY: Peace Hill, Francis Bay, Yawzi Point, Maho Goat, Trunk Underwater

15 - 30 MINUTES ONE WAY: Water Catchment, Turtle Point, Cinnamon Nature, America Hill, Leinster Bay, Drunk Bay, Europa Bay, Dittlif Point

30 - 60 MINUTES ONE WAY: Lind Point, Caneel Hill, Ram Head, Cinnamon Bay, Lameshur, Bordeaux Mountain, Little Reef Bay

MORE THAN 60 MINUTES ONE WAY: Margaret Hill, Johnny Horn, Brown Bay, Reef Bay

EASY TRAILS: Peace Hill, Francis Bay, Drunk Bay, Cinnamon Nature Trail, Yawzi Point Trail, Leinster Bay

DIFFICULT TRAILS: Johnny Horn, Brown Bay, Bordeaux Mountain, Margaret Hill, Little Reef Bay

HISTORIC SITES ON TRAIL: Peace Hill, America Hill, Johnny Horn, Brown Bay, Reef Bay

BEACH ALONG THE WAY: Lind Point, Turtle Point, Francis Bay, Brown Bay, Johnny Horn, Bordeaux Mountain, Drunk Bay, Ram Head, Yawzi Point, Lameshur, Europa Bay, Reef Bay, Dittlif Point, Little Reef Bay Trail

UNDERWATER TRAIL: Trunk Bay

TRAILS FROM CRUZ BAY: Lind Point, Caneel Hill, Margaret Hill

ON THE BUS LINE: Water Catchment, Cinnamon Bay, Reef Bay, Johnny Horn, Drunk Bay, Ram Head

RENTAL CAR REQUIRED TO REACH: Brown Bay, Bordeaux Mountain, Yawzi Point, Lameshur, Europa, Dittlif Point, Leinster Bay, Little Reef Bay

NORTH SHORE TRAILS: Lind Point, Caneel Hill, Margaret Hill, Water Catchment, Turtle Point, Peace Hill, Trunk Underwater, Cinnamon Nature, Cinnamon Bay, America Hill, Maho Goat, Francis Bay, Leinster Bay, Johnny

Horn, Brown Bay

SALT POND ROAD TRAILS: Drunk Bay, Ram Head, Yawzi Point, Lameshur, Bordeaux Mountain, Europa Bay

EAST END ROAD TRAILS: Johnny Horn, Brown Bay

CENTERLINE ROAD TRAILS: Water Catchment, Cinnamon Bay, Reef Bay, Bordeaux Mountain Road

SOUTH SHORE TRAILS: Dittlif Point, Little Reef Bay Trail

TRAIL LOOPS: (1) Cruz Bay, Caneel Hill, Lind Point, Cruz Bay
(2) Cruz Bay, Caneel Hill, Margaret Hill, Lind Point, Cruz Bay
(3) Cinnamon Bay, Centerline Road, John's Head Road, North Shore Road

DROP OFF / PICK UP HIKES: Bordeaux Mountain, Johnny Horn, Brown Bay, Cinnamon Bay, Little Reef Bay then up the Reef Bay Trail

BEST TRAILS: Cinnamon Nature Trail, Reef Bay, Ram Head

If you want to get a little wilder, see the next chapter for "Off the Trail" hikes.

## TRAILS IN DETAIL

# TRAILS LESS THAN 15 MINUTES ONE WAY

### PEACE HILL TRAIL

Peace Hill Trail starts from a parking lot on the North Shore Road just past Easter Rock. The short trail leads to Peace Hill, some windmill ruins, and a spectacular view of the entire North Shore (but you will no longer find the famous Christ of the Caribbean statue). Return to the parking lot on the same trail.

From the parking lot, follow the trail up the hill (the cactus on the right is Night Blooming Cereus – worth coming back to see one evening during the blooming season – if you see any closed up flowers, now is the right time), past the windmill ruins, onto the plateau – what a view!

The windmill ruins offer a bit of shade along with a close-up look at the beautiful traditional stonework. There is a very active honeybee population that is working on recreating the enormous hive which was destroyed by the same storm that took down the statue. Look for them high up on the wall where a stone fell out. The bees happily fly out over the top and probably won't bother you unless you make them mad.

Colonel Wadsworth donated this land to the National Park and in 1953 put up a big white concrete statue of the Christ of the Caribbean. It was not a particularly beautiful statue, (especially since one of the arms that were raised to the sky kept breaking off, so they just broke off the other arm and left it like that), but it became a locally famous landmark. The National Park did not like the statue but the Colonel's bequest specifically stated that the statue could not be removed. After surviving a few hurricanes, it finally got knocked down and of course, the Park will not replace it. Instead they installed a little plaque.

Upon his recent death after a long wait (he donated it in his sixties but didn't die until in his nineties), the Park also gained control over the rest of the Colonel's bequest – the Denis Bay Plantation. But there are some very complicated leases and rules still in effect that means the Park still doesn't really have absolute control and it is not OK for you to go strolling down the driveway to Denis Bay.

There is an unofficial turnoff to the right about 2 minutes up this trail from the parking lot, which leads to the far end of Denis Bay beach (about 10 minutes). This trail is not maintained, so you might get scratched up, and please do not trespass on the private property at the far right-hand side of the beach. Snorkeling around Perkins Cay (the little island just off shore) is very nice.

## MAHO GOAT TRAIL

From Maho Beach, this steep trail leads to the Maho Bay Campground. It is a short cut for campers, since getting there by road involves an extra couple of miles and taxi drivers refuse to go on the dirt road to the campground. One way hiking time is 15 minutes. The trail starts at the far end of Maho Beach, just before the North Shore Road turns sharply inland to the right. It ends at the Maho Bay Campground's front desk.

## FRANCIS BAY TRAIL

The Francis Bay Trail starts from the parking area near a nice old stone warehouse on the Maho Bay Campground Road. It wanders about half a mile through the forest, past more ruins, around a salt pond, then leads to Francis Bay Beach. A new section of the trail then heads back into the bush to follow the perimeter of the salt pond and ends up in the Francis Bay Beach parking lot. Return the same way or follow the dirt road out to the Maho Bay Campground Road. One way hiking time to the beach is about 15 minutes. The new section hiking time is also about 15 minutes.

This mostly flat nature trail is excellent for bird watching. Since birds love to eat bugs, you can expect plenty of both in the morning and late afternoon. The Audubon Society features this trail in the *Birds of the Caribbean* book, and the National Park offers a Bird Hike in season that I highly recommend (tell Ranger Laurel I sent you). A portion of the trail near the salt pond is a boardwalk.

## YAWZI TRAIL

The Yawzi Trail starts from the road to the VIERS lab (Virgin Islands Environmental Research Station), which is off the Lameshur Road (Lameshur Road requires four-wheel drive to negotiate, see page 120 for details). The mostly flat trail goes out around the point, and you return on the same trail. Hiking time is about 15 minutes one way.

The Yawzi Trail goes out to Yawzi Point, through a dry forest. If you look very hard, you can find ruins of the Yawzi Quarantine camp. Yawzi is an African disease, similar to leprosy, that came over with the slaves. The method of treatment back then was to send all the infected people out to this point and leave them there until they died. Along the trail is a little rocky beach on the Great Lameshur Bay side. This is an excellent snorkeling take-off point for experienced snorkelers: enter the water here, then go right following the reefs and coral heads around the point. Pay attention to currents and waves as you round the point. You could keep snorkeling all the way around the peninsula past lots of spectacular reefs, but it's a long way, with no other convenient exit point until Lameshur Bay beach.

## TRUNK BAY UNDERWATER TRAIL

This is a snorkeling trail, starting at Trunk Bay Beach, which is on the North

Shore Road. The trail starts at a big round white buoy in the water directly in front of the lifeguard stand. Follow the underwater signs out to the big red buoy, and then back to the big blue buoy – it's a big triangle. Swimming distance is about 150 yards, time required to swim the trail ranges from 10 minutes to an hour depending on how enthralled you get by the fish and coral. You do not have to stay on the trail and you can snorkel it in both directions. (For more beach details see page 40).

# TRAILS 15 TO 30 MINUTES ONE WAY

## TURTLE POINT TRAIL

The Turtle Point Trail is a National Park Trail within the Caneel Resort grounds. Caneel Bay has decided to call it the Mary Rockefeller trail since she donated some fancy benches at the lookout points. It is a circular trail with some hill-climbing that takes about 30 minutes to hike. There are very nice benches scattered along the trail at the best viewpoints. Caneel Resort asks that you stop at the front desk to sign in as a day guest and pick up a trail map. Tell the resort shuttle bus driver where you want to go and he will drop you off at the trail starting point. The trail follows the water around the point of the Caneel peninsula, goes through a forest and out to rocky cliffs which offer excellent views of the North Shore cays and islands. This is a great place to sit and watch the sailboats do battle with the very strong current. Many times the current is stronger than the wind and the boats end up sailing backwards until they give up and start their engine (if they have one). The trail continues to Turtle Bay Beach where you can go for a swim before catching a shuttle back to the parking area. (See the Update Chapter for more information about the Turtle Point Trail).

## CINNAMON BAY NATURE TRAIL

The Cinnamon Bay Nature Trail starts behind the Cinnamon Bay Ruins located on the opposite side of the North Shore Road from the campground. Park along the road or in the campground parking lot. To find where the trail starts, follow the self-guided tour through the ruins until you are behind the last building. At the far end of the building is a sign pointing out the trail. Be sure you have gone through the ruins to get to this trail, another much longer trail (Cinnamon Bay Trail) starts from the road without going through the ruins.

The circular Cinnamon Bay Nature Trail has signs identifying different trees and plants along the way and a stop at the plantation cemetery. This beautiful, short, almost flat trail follows a "gut" (a river bed that is usually dry), up one side and returns along the other through the semi-tropical dry forest. Walking time about ½ hour.

## AMERICA HILL TRAIL

The America Hill Trail is a spur from the Cinnamon Bay Trail. The Cinnamon Bay Trail starts on the North Shore Road to the left of the Cinnamon Bay Ruins across the road from the campground. Hiking time one way is about 30 minutes, return the same way or continue on the Cinnamon Bay Trail to Centerline Road.

Start climbing the Cinnamon Bay Trail (hang in there, the first 5 minutes are the worst of it). About 10 minutes along the trail, just after you cross the dry riverbed, the trail to America Hill goes off to the left of the main trail. There is a metal post that used to have a sign on it but the Park Service took it down because the America Hill Great House ruins are dangerous. They are not encouraging people to go up there, and so they quit maintaining the trail. This means it could be hard to find the trail if no one has used it recently. But if you are determined to go anyway, it's a 20-minute hard climb up to the house. Don't be stupid and climb around inside – the basement is a good 20 feet down and all that collapsed, rusty, galvanized roofing is not going to support your weight.

Walk around the whole house, the view from the far side is magnificent. There were plans to try to restore this house, but then Hurricane Hugo totally demolished the roof, so it would cost too much to fix now. The St. John Historical Society comes up here once in a while and clears the bush around a few of the smaller buildings and the flagpole area, so hunt around and see what you can find. When the house was occupied, they did not have to walk up that trail because there was a road that went down to Maho Bay on that side of the hill.

## WATER CATCHMENT TRAIL

The Water Catchment Trail starts from Centerline Road near the dump, then winds easily down the hill to the North Shore Road up the hill from the Caneel entrance. One way hiking time is about 30 minutes, longer to return going uphill.

Where Centerline Road swings in a wide curve around the dump, there is a small dirt area to park. It is 1.5 miles from Cruz Bay on the left-hand side. (At the moment there is no sign, possibly because they finally realized that the last sign wrongly identified this trail as the Caneel Trail).

The Water Catchment Trail is the most direct way to get to the North Shore Road, and it's downhill all the way. However, bear in mind that not too many people use this trail, so it might be a little bushy.

The trail meanders through the forest along the slopes of the gut leading to the large reservoir, which was Caneel's sole source water until they got their reverse osmosis plant installed. The trail continues along the dirt access road down the hill to connect with the North Shore Road.

Along the way there are two opportunities to end up on the Caneel and Margaret Hills Trail. The exact location of these intersections change with each major storm, but don't worry: if you end up at an intersection with a much larger trail, just remember that uphill goes to Margaret and Caneel Hills, and downhill goes to the North Shore Road.

Very close to Centerline Road is the first intersection on the left which takes you to Margaret Hill. The second intersection is about 10 minutes down the trail. About half the way along the reservoir, to the left, is where another intersection used to be but it never got cleared after Hurricane Marilyn. This is the intersection that is on all of the Park's official maps, and signs mark it at both ends but it is extremely difficult to get through (wild pineapple plants plus very thick thorny bushes – you will get scratched up).

The middle section of the reservoir is for holding the water; all around the edges and up the hills are to catch the rain – thus the name 'water catchment.' Recently the dam was closed, the concrete showed signs of being patched, and water was being circulated with a pump. I hope that means someone is going to make use of this water source again to help solve our constant water shortage problem.

At the reservoir the trail joins the access road and wanders gently down the hill to the pump station and the North Shore Road. Turn left to go down the hill to the Caneel entrance, or turn right to go to Hawksnest Beach.

You can return the same way or flag down a taxi to go back to Cruz Bay. Or you can hike the Caneel and Margaret Hills Trail back to Cruz Bay (90 minutes, hard climbing). Or you can walk to Caneel Bay Beach (10 minutes), and then follow the Lind Point Trail back to Cruz Bay (45 minutes easy climbing).

## DRUNK BAY TRAIL

The Drunk Bay Trail starts at the far end of Salt Pond Bay Beach, behind the trees. If you head over to the salt pond behind the beach, you'll find the trail skirting the pond's edge. If it's been raining a lot, the trail may be slightly underwater in a few spots. Salt Pond is one foot below sea level, the lowest point on St. John.

This pond is still used by some to collect salt. During dry spells, the seawater that seeps in from under the ground evaporates. This leaves a white crust of sea salt crystals that is easy to scoop up. The red tint in the water is algae.

The trail continues through this very dry area, leaving the pond and crossing over to the ocean. The coastline here is wild and rugged, not good for swimming, but great for beachcombing. Return the same way you came. Hiking time about 20 minutes one way. (For details about the beach see page 47.) It is possible to continue hiking along the coast, scramble around the cliffs and reach Concordia Campground. This is a long, hot hike.

## EUROPA BAY TRAIL

On the Lameshur Trail, the turnoff to Europa Bay is on the left about 0.3 miles down the trail. The Lameshur Trail starts at the end of the Lameshur Road which requires four-wheel drive to negotiate. Hiking time one way from the parking area is 30 minutes.

The Lameshur Trail starts on the other side of the chain at the parking area, and then climbs slowly. The turnoff to Europa is marked with a sign. Follow the trail down the hill to a large salt pond with lots of ducks and water birds who obviously don't like being disturbed, then to a rocky beach.

Just before you get to the beach, look for wild orchids growing in the trees and on the ground (please don't pick them). Three of St. John's five types of wild orchids grow here in this hostile environment. These delicate plants are so close to the sea that they regularly get drenched with salt spray – yet they are thriving.

Europa Bay has small reefs, but the waves can make snorkeling here dangerous. At the far right end of the beach is White Point. These are some spectacular white cliffs that are only noticeable from the sea. There isn't any trail along the cliffs which is just as well, as it looks like a good place to hurt yourself. (For beach details see page 49.)

## DITTLIF POINT TRAIL

Dittlif Point has been developed, so now there is a paved road instead of a trail. Sometimes you can drive down the road, but officially you cannot. So I will continue to treat it as a walking trail. Dittlif Point Trail starts on the Fish Bay Road. It takes about 20 minutes to hike one way. The trail branches out to beaches on either side of the peninsula and involves some mild hill-climbing. There is no shade. Make sure that you bring some water, as this is a hot, dry hike.

From the parking area on Fish Bay Road, follow the road through the hot, dry forest until you see the paths branching off – 1.) Left goes to a stony beach on the Fish Bay side, 2.) Right goes down to the beach on the Rendezvous Bay side, 3.) Straight continues out to Dittlif Hill and the top of the cliffs on the point and to another beach on the Fish Bay side.

The Fish Bay beaches are reputed to have excellent snorkeling. The center trail out to the point involves some climbing to get to the top of Dittlif Hill, but the views are worth it. The beach on the Rendezvous Bay side has some sand, more rocks, and the water is almost all sea grass. The trail continues past the beach and follows along the rock pools out to the point. Rock climbers might be able to scramble up and around to the other side, but it's a lot easier to just go back the way you came after you've had your fill of watching the waves crash through the various crevasses. Snorkeling the reefs around this point can be dangerous unless the water is very calm. At about the middle of the beach there is a 5-foot tall cairn (rocks stacked in a column) marking a small shortcut back up to the trail going to Dittlif Hill and the cliffs. I don't know how long the cairn will stay stacked there, but someone deserves congratulations for a beautiful construction job. A friend and business associate of Mr. Rockefeller was given this entire peninsula as a thank-you for his help in buying up 2/3 of St. John back in the 1950's. (For detail on the beaches see page 55.)

## LEINSTER BAY TRAIL

The Leinster Bay Trail starts at Annaberg, following what was a dirt road along the coast. It leads to a nice little beach, the beginning of the Johnny Horn Trail, and the closest spot to swim over to Waterlemon Cay. There is very good snorkeling all along this trail.

# TRAILS 30 to 60 MINUTES ONE WAY

## LIND POINT TRAIL

This nice, easy, well-maintained trail starts in Cruz Bay, goes out to Lind Point, then around to Salomon and Honeymoon beaches and ends at Caneel Bay Beach. Actually this is no longer one trail: due to heavy local usage there is now an upper route and a lower route. Both end up in the same place and are the same length.

It takes about 25 minutes to hike to Salomon, another 20 minutes to get to Caneel and 5 minutes to get taxied back to Cruz Bay. Another possible return trip is to walk through Caneel Resort to the North Shore Road and hike the steep Caneel Hill Trail back to Cruz Bay.

The Lind Point Trail starts in Cruz Bay behind the National Park Visitors Center Building. Go to the parking lot behind the building and look for the trail marker sign. Scramble up the hill to a good size dirt road (this is the road to our seaplane airport – too bad Hurricane Hugo sank all the planes, and when some decided to start up the seaplanes again, the Park refused them access to the ramp). The trail continues directly across this road and soon widens. After a bit, the lower route turns off to the left. The upper route continues straight up the easy climb to the top where a bench is waiting for you at the Lind Point Overlook. After watching the ferries and admiring the view of Pillsbury Sound, continue walking around the point to the left hand turnoff down a fairly steep hill to the lower route and then on to Salomon Beach. If you continue straight, the trail leads to Caneel Resort but so does the trail to Salomon and Honeymoon.

Salomon Beach is a white sandy beach lined with coconut palms. It is a great place for swimming and the snorkeling is pretty good. Because it can only be reached by hiking, this has become St. John's unofficial "clothing optional" beach. If this would offend you, please continue on to Honeymoon Beach where they keep their clothes on. (Nudity is against the laws of the VI.)

At the far end of Salomon, the trail continues. The path goes up a small hill through the grounds of what used to be the Presidential Suite of the Caneel Resorts. Lots of U.S. Presidents stayed here, as well as Mr. Rockefeller. It has been turned over to the National Park, who turned it into housing for some important employee. (For more beach details see page 38.)

## CANEEL HILL TRAIL

The Caneel Hill Trail is one section of the Caneel Hill and Margaret Hill Trail. To hike both trails requires about 90 miles of very steep climbing. It runs from the North Shore Road in Cruz Bay to the North Shore Road at the Caneel entrance.

The trail starts just passed the Mongoose Junction complex in Cruz Bay. The sign is right next to the telephone pole, hidden in the bushes.

The Caneel Hill portion of the trail takes about 30 to 40 minutes to climb from Cruz Bay. It is fairly steep. At the top of Caneel Hill (elevation 719 feet) are spectacular views of St. John, St. Thomas, St. Croix, the Puerto Rican islands of

Culebra and Vieques, Jost Van Dyke (BVI), and about 20 other small cays (the wooden lookout tower blew away and has not yet been replaced, but "any day now" it will be). The reward is well worth the sweaty hike.

To return, continue on the Margaret Hill Trail (see page 73) or go back the way you came to the marked spur tail which leads across the North Shore Road at the road to the Biosphere. This spur trail leads down to the Lind Point Trail that goes back to Cruz Bay (and branches off to Salomon and Honeymoon beaches).

## CINNAMON BAY TRAIL

The Cinnamon Bay Trail starts at the North Shore Road and climbs steadily up to Centerline Road. Hiking time one way is about 60 minutes. This trail makes a good drop-off/pick-up hike: get dropped off on Centerline Road then hike (all downhill) to Cinnamon Bay where you can meet your party or catch a taxi back to Cruz Bay. Another way to do this trail is to use John Head Road for the return trip: Starting at Cinnamon, hike up to Centerline, turn right and walk along the road to John's Head Road, stop and visit the Catherineburg Ruins, then follow the dirt road down to the North Shore Road. Turn right and continue back to Cinnamon Bay.

The Cinnamon Bay hiking trail starts to the left of the Cinnamon Bay Ruins across the road from the campground. The first 5 minutes are the worst part of the whole trail – very steep and not well-shaded. After that the going gets somewhat easier, but it is a steady climb all the way up to Centerline Road, following an old plantation road. About 10 minutes along the trail – just after you cross the dry riverbed – the trail to America Hill goes off to the left of the main trail. The trail continues to climb along the edge of the very wide valley. During the plantation days this whole area was cultivated, so all the trees here are a secondary forest.

## RAM HEAD TRAIL

The Ram Head Trail starts at the end of Salt Pond Bay Beach and goes out to the southernmost point of St. John. This is a hot, dry hike, but well worth the effort. Make sure you bring some water and remember to protect yourself from the sun. Hiking time is 45 minutes one way.

The Ram Head trail follows the rocky shore past the left end of the Salt Pond beach for a little ways, and then turns inland. It may not always be marked well, but just look around and follow the most defined path. After leaving the shoreline, the trail climbs slowly up and over a small hill through the very dry cactus forest. On the other side of this hill, past the rope swing, is the long rocky Ram Head Trail Beach. The rocks make walking a little difficult, so take your time. Aren't the colorful rocks, tumbled so smooth by the ocean, just beautiful?

This is a good spot to take a swim or snorkel, but watch out for sea urchins. The trail follows the rocky beach almost to the end, then look for where the path starts to climb up the hill. It switches back and forth, passing by roly-poly cactus with their red hats (Barrel Cactus, the fuchsia fruits are edible), until you get to the saddle. Now, hold onto your hat, your kids or any lightweight people, because the wind here can easily blow them away. Don't get too close to the edge; erosion is currently in progress, but do look down into the crevasse and check out the waves crashing. A little further on is another crevasse, just as spectacular. Turn around and a look along the south shore. The fault line can be clearly seen – some of the points have already lost their ends to erosion. On some others, like this one, the water is still in the process of crashing through the cliff and creating a little island that in turn will be eroded until it vanishes. Keep walking until you get to the top of Ram Head (altitude 196 feet), the southernmost point on St. John. There is a mystical feeling up here, like there should be Stonehenge-type monuments and sacred rites being performed, but usually the only activity is some goats playing on the cliffs. Hiking up here during the full moon is magical, but difficult – in ideal conditions, the moon provides just enough light to follow the trail. If clouds block the moonlight, you will need a good flashlight.

## LAMESHUR BAY TRAIL

The Lameshur Bay Trail starts at the end of Lameshur Road (a four-wheel drive road), goes past the turnoff to Europa Bay (.3 miles), climbing slowly up and over a large hill to connect with the Reef Bay Trail (1.8 miles). One way hiking time is 60 minutes. Add on 30 minutes each way to go see the Reef Bay petroglyphs, the Reef Bay Great House or the Reef Bay Ruins and beach.

From the parking lot at the end of the Lameshur Road, hop across the chain to start the trail (don't go up the dirt road instead – that leads to the Rangers house and the Bordeaux Mountain Trail).

The turnoff to the Great House is unmarked, and since there has been a lot of activity lately, it looks like the main trail. When you get to the Y-junction, right takes you up a steep switchback hill to the house; left takes you down hill to connect with the Reef Bay trail. At that intersection, left will take you to the ruins and the beach; right goes to the petroglyph turnoff and back up to Centerline Road. Using the Lameshur Trail to get to Reef Bay is not any quicker or easier than taking the Reef Bay Trail.

## BORDEAUX MOUNTAIN TRAIL

Bordeaux Mountain Trail starts on Bordeaux Mountain Road and ends at Little Lameshur Beach, dropping 1277 feet in 1.2 miles. It's steep. It takes about 60 minutes to hike down, much longer to hike up. This trail is a lot more fun to hike if you can get someone to drop you off at the top, then while you hike, they drive around to meet you at Lameshur Beach. Hitchhiking from Lameshur is very difficult because not very many people go there.

To find the trail, drive on Bordeaux Mountain Road for 1.7 miles (this means you go past the end of the paved part). Look for a telephone pole labeled ES50 on the right side. The trail begins just past that pole. You might be able to see the trail sign if someone has pruned the bushes recently.  Before you start down the hill, take a minute to go across the road to check out the extensive ruins. Isn't it a shame that the engineers decided that the road had to cut through one corner of the ruins?

The Bordeaux Mountain Trail is the old plantation road that connected the plantation at the top with the plantation at the bottom. It follows along the ridge of a magnificent valley, with very few trees overhanging the trail which makes for excellent views and lots of sun on your head. Oxen pulling heavy wagons had to be able to make it up and down the hill so the grade is not extremely steep, but it's long and steady, no flat spots at all. Close to the bottom, the trail comes out onto a dirt road; to the left takes you to the Rangers house, straight down takes you to Lameshur Beach where you can cool off with a long swim before hiking back up.

**LITTLE REEF BAY TRAIL**
There is a half-official, half-unofficial trail called the Little Reef Bay Trail that allows you to get to the Reef Bay Trail from Fish Bay (about 40 minutes one way). This trail is difficult and requires some scrambling.

Find the very steep trail down to Parret Bay on the Reef Bay Road (see page 55). Follow the beach to the rocks at the far left end, where it is possible – not easy, but possible – to walk around the rocky point if the waves are not too rough. If the waves are too big you will need to give up and return the way you came. (Please do not ruin your vacation by insisting that you are bigger and stronger than large waves).

Once around the point, continue walking down the sandy Little Reef Bay beach. About 25 feet before the end of the sand, look in the bushes for the trail going up and over the hill to end up on the Reef Bay Trail at the sugar mill ruins. This is also the best place for swimming and where to start snorkeling out to the reef.

The Virgin Islands Audubon Society sells an expensive, but neat little booklet *Little Reef Bay Trail*, available at Connections, about the birds, plants, and sea life to be found, history of the area, and an explanation of the ruins that are located in the very heavy bush behind the beach.

# TRAILS: MORE THAN 60 MINUTES ONE WAY

### MARGARET HILL TRAIL

The steep and long Margaret Hill Trail starts in Cruz Bay and climbs to the summit of Caneel Hill as part of the Caneel Hill Trail, continues to the summit of Margaret Hill, then descends to the North Shore Road at the Caneel Bay entrance. It intersects with the Water Catchment Trail in two places (despite what the National Park map says). Hiking time is at least 90 minutes one way. To return to Cruz Bay you can return the same way or flag down a taxi. Another option is to walk to Caneel Bay Beach and hike the Lind Point Trail back to Cruz Bay. A third possibility is to hike the Water Catchment Trail up to Centerline Road and then hitchhike back to Cruz Bay.

The Caneel Hill Trail starts in Cruz Bay just past the Mongoose Junction complex on the right. Past the end of the stone wall, right next to the telephone pole, look for a sign hidden in the bushes, identifying the Caneel Hill and Margaret Hill Trails. The trail climbs steeply up the hill to the summit of Caneel Hill (719 feet) where the views are excellent. (This is the perfect spot to use a panoramic camera.)

The trail then descends Caneel Hill. At the bottom is a large Tamarind tree and a bench with a trail sign. Directly across the trail from the sign is an unofficial trail down to the North Shore Road. The official trail continuing up to Margaret Hill is not always easy to follow. These trails are used by people going to work at the Caneel Bay Resort, and they don't want to have to climb Margaret Hill to get there. Any trails going off to the left are unofficial trails to the North Shore Road. There is only one unofficial trail going off to the right that might confuse you. It is about 2 minutes past the Tamarind tree. If you end up directly above a blue roof and see a U.S. Boundary sign – go back to the main trail. Otherwise, just don't take any left turns and keep heading uphill. Almost at the summit of Margaret Hill is a large rock outcropping with spectacular views. Below you is the section of St. John we call Pastory, and those are the Pastory Estate Condos.

This is a good place to take a break and congratulate yourself. It's about 2 minutes further to the top of Margaret Hill, and then it's all downhill.

After a number of switchbacks, there is an unmarked trail off to the right. This leads to the Water Catchment Trail (see page 66). Further down the hill is a marked intersection with the same trail. Eventually the Margaret Hill Trail comes to the North Shore Road at the Caneel entrance.

### JOHNNY HORN TRAIL

The Johnny Horn Trail starts at the **Moravian Church** in Coral Bay and ends at Waterlemon Beach or vice versa. The bus can drop you off in front of the church. Hiking time is 90 minutes one-way and it's a long, hot difficult hike on the unmaintained trail. Return the same way, or even better, do this as a pick-up/drop-off hike. Get dropped off at the Moravian Church in Coral Bay, and then hike the unmaintained trail over to Waterlemon beach where the rest of your group has been snorkeling while you've been sweating up and down the hills. If you are relying on hitchhiking to get back, it might be easier to get dropped off on the Annaberg side and hike to Coral Bay.

The driveway of the Moravian Church is the trailhead for the Johnny Horn Trail. Follow the dirt road up the long, long hill; don't take any of the right-hand forks. At the top of this hill the road ends and the trail begins. This used to be a well-traveled road, to and from the small settlement of Johnny Horn before Mr. Rockefeller bought up the land and gave it to the Park, so it's an easy grade and a pretty wide trail. The trail is not maintained by the National Park but currently the trail is getting enough traffic from people and donkeys to keep the Ketch-N-Keep from taking over.

The trail goes over a lot of hills and there is very little shade. About halfway down what looks like the final descent (there's one more little hill to climb) the Brown Bay Trail turns off to the right to descend to Brown Bay Beach. Continue straight down the main trail and at the crest of what really is the last hill, there is another turnoff to the right that leads to the ruins of the Boy's Home. This beautiful old estate house, built on the ruins of the Danish fort, was used not too long ago as a home for boys. The location would certainly keep them from sneaking out to go into town! The patio of the house offers wonderful views of Drake's Passage and the British Virgin Islands.

Back on the main trail, it's only another 10 minutes to the bottom and Waterlemon Beach, and the Leinster Bay Trail out to the Annaberg Road where hopefully someone is waiting to give you a ride so you don't have to hike all the way back.

### BROWN BAY TRAIL

The Brown Bay Trail starts on the East End Road and goes over the hill to Brown Bay Beach, then goes back up a long hill to join the Johnny Horn Trail and descend to Waterlemon Beach. The trail is not maintained by the National Park but currently the trail is getting enough traffic from people and donkeys to keep the Ketch-N-Keep from taking over (Nice work everyone!). Hiking time is about 90 minutes, add more time for snorkeling.

Brown Bay Beach is the high point of this trail and is located not quite halfway along the trail (it is a little closer to the East End Road side of the trail, about a 20-minute walk). The bay offers excellent snorkeling. There are plenty of baby conchs in the sea grass beds and good reefs to snorkel.

You can start this hike from either the East End Road or Waterlemon Beach and return by hiking the same way. Even better, get someone to drop you off on the East End Road. While you are hiking, they can go snorkeling at Waterlemon Beach until you get there. Hitchhiking from either end is going to be difficult.

If there is a problem with getting dropped off, you could start in Coral Bay, hike the Johnny Horn Trail to the Brown Bay turnoff, go down to Brown Bay and follow that trail to Hurricane Hole, then hike along the East End Road back to Coral Bay. This would be a really long, hot, difficult hike, but, hey! it's your vacation.

Just past Estate Zootenvaal and over the bridge on the East End Road is a dirt road to the left that leads to the Hermitage ruins and the beginning of the Brown Bay Trail. Follow the road up the hill, visit the ruins if you like, then keep climbing. If you hear gunshots, don't worry. No one is after you. The police do their target practice in this area. The Brown Bay Trail continues up and over the hill then descends to Brown Bay Beach and Salt Pond. After your snorkel stop, get back on the trail in the same place. There is no way to take a shortcut from the far end of the beach – the salt pond is in the way and you'll end up heading in the wrong direction. The official trail goes around the salt pond that is full of birds and ducks, and then starts climbing up Leinster Hill to join up with the Johnny Horn Trail at the top. Turn right to continue on to Waterlemon, left to hike the Johnny Horn Trail back to Coral Bay (For beach detail see page 50).

It is possible to follow the coastline from Brown Bay around to Waterlemon – difficult but possible. There is no trail. You have to scramble over the boulders that line the shore. If you twist an ankle, or worse, it is going to be really hard to get you out. If you are up to it, this is a very nice scramble, with good beachcombing and some nice reefs to snorkel if it isn't too rough.

Scattered along the Brown Bay Trail are clothes and shoes (check the labels – Chinese!). We are the final stop on a long voyage to smuggle Chinese citizens into the US (they pay about $30,000 for this trip). On this isolated coastline, the passengers jump overboard and swim to shore carrying a set of dry clothes in a plastic bag. They change into the dry clothes, abandon the wet ones, hike to the nearest road, and then try hard to be "found" by the police quickly (this is pretty easy – it is impossible for 30 Chinese to stroll through Coral Bay without being noticed). Once arrested, they apply for asylum and are given food and water and transported to Puerto Rico where an attorney is waiting for them to arrive. St. John could really use a Chinese restaurant – maybe a few of these illegal aliens will get lost one day and stay here. Sometimes the cargo is Haitians or Dominica Republicans – they cannot apply for asylum and do not want to be found.

## REEF BAY TRAIL

The Reef Bay Trail is an excellent hike that starts at Centerline Road. It descends to the petroglyphs and waterfall, the Reef Bay Great House, the sugar factory, and to Reef Bay Beach.

The National Park offers a guided tour of this trail once or twice a week. (Sign up well in advance. For more information, contact the NPS Visitors Center in Cruz Bay at 776-6201).

With the tour, not only do you get a ranger to tell you all about everything, you avoid walking back up the hill because a boat meets you at the beach to return you to Cruz Bay.

The trail has signs all along the way identifying plants, trees, animals, ruins, petroglyphs, the history of the Reef Bay plantation and how the sugar mill operated – so you don't absolutely need a guide. Hiking time is about 1 ½ hours one way for just the trail, at least another ½ hour to 1 hour for the side trips. It is possible to do all this in half a day, but this trail offers so much that it's much better to pack a lunch, your snorkel, and make a day of it.

Please Note: there is no snack bar anywhere along this trail and the water at the waterfall is not drinkable. This wonderful hike will be a total disaster if you don't take plenty of water.

The Reef Bay Trail is about two miles long (did you notice that every sign stating mileage on this trail adds up to a different total number of miles?). It is all downhill going in, and all uphill coming back – but the first half mile is the steepest and it's not that bad, just take your time. The top portion of the Reef Bay gut is one of the few places on the island where the original native trees were left uncut. At the bottom of the hill, just as the trail flattens out, is the signed turnoff to the right to the waterfall pool and the petroglyphs (pictures carved into the rocks). It's a short detour and well worth it. The waterfall is usually not running unless there's been a lot of rain but the pool never dries up. Be sure to take the time to look in the pool, at lots of interesting little water bugs, fish, crayfish and dragonflies; splash water on the rocks to make the petroglyphs show up better.

The very, very, very steep trail to the left of the waterfall leads to the top of the cliff (what a view!) and also to the two other waterfalls further up the gut. The National Park does NOT want anyone to use this trail because it is so dangerous. (You've been warned!)

Back on the main Reef Bay Trail, the turnoff to the left goes to the Reef Bay Great House and to the Lameshur Bay Trail. Keep going straight, following along the mangrove swamp and you'll get to the sugar mill ruins and then the beach. Directly across from the ruins is the turnoff for the Little Reef Bay Trail which will take you to Parret Bay Beach and eventually, after some rock scrambling, comes out at the Fish Bay Road.

The sugar mill ruins are well-marked so that you can understand how the mill worked. Be sure to look up – fruit bats live here. Also go outside and around the corner to find the steam engine and the large honeybee hive.

The Lady Bird Johnson latrine (she was horrified that there were no facilities and got this one built) is not maintained very often – please do not make it worse by using it as a trash barrel.

You might have to search around a little to find the trail to the beach (the clearing crew was instructed to clear to the ruins and that is exactly what they did, not an inch further) but you can figure it out. After all that hiking, a nice cool swim would feel great, but surprise – the bay is so shallow that the water temperature is usually about the same as your body temperature! The swimming is good straight out; snorkeling can be done on the outside of the reef to the left or the rocks to the right. (For more beach details see page 49.)

## REEF BAY GREAT HOUSE

When you are refreshed, go back the way you came on the trail until you get to the Lameshur Trail turnoff on your right. Take that, and at the T-intersection, go left, winding around the switchbacks until you get to the Reef Bay Great House (also known as the Par Force House). Ever so often the National Park does a little bit more restoration to keep this house from falling apart. The architecture is magnificent and the view is well worth the climb (see the waterfall on the other side of the valley?). The house was lived-in as recently as the 1950's. Actually, the last person to live here was a woman named Anna Marsh. She was murdered on the premises. (A stolen brooch led to her killer's arrest.)

The restoration process is in three phases: the first, tear down the southwest corner, put a stable foundation down, then build it back up using the original bricks. This was completed in 1992. That section of the house was built using the walls of a very old structure that did not have a good foundation. (It was sinking, and pulling all the walls down with it.)

The second phase is in progress now, whenever funds are available. It is to fix the roof and the exterior until it is weatherproof (they finished that part years ago), and then restore the exterior to its original condition (no sign of this part starting yet). The third phase is not yet approved for funding, but it will be to restore the interior and the gardens.

The restoration process has had its ups and downs – literally. On the first attempt, all the material had been gathered and helicopters borrowed to fly it all in, but the very expensive generator was dropped into the sea and the project was abandoned. After many years, they were finally ready to try again. This time the Lameshur Trail was cleared temporarily so that the workmen could get in, and the Navy helicopters that hauled the materials flew over land only and didn't drop anything (but everyone in Coral Bay ducked that day).

The restoration process is done by special National Park masons and carpenters whose job is to travel around all the National Parks in the U.S. fixing old structures. They are assisted by unskilled volunteers from the community. If they ever start working again (ask at the National Park Visitors Center) and you want to do something really different on your vacation, why not volunteer for a day?

When you are ready to go down, follow the same trail out but look for a small unofficial trail off to the right at the last switchback (on the side closest to the valley). If you miss it, just go back to the Reef Bay Trail the same way you came. If you found it, this is the (unmaintained) trail which is shown on the official VI National Park map. The Park does NOT want people to use this trail. It leads down to some ruins of a small distillery and some slave quarters, then intersects with the Reef Bay Trail.

Now it's time to hike back up the hill to Centerline Road. This does not have to be a miserable experience – just take your time. If you are hiking with someone determined to break a speed record, tell them to either slow down or go ahead without you. If they push really hard, they could make it to the car, go to Chateau Bordeaux and meet you back at the trailhead with an ice cream or a cold beer.

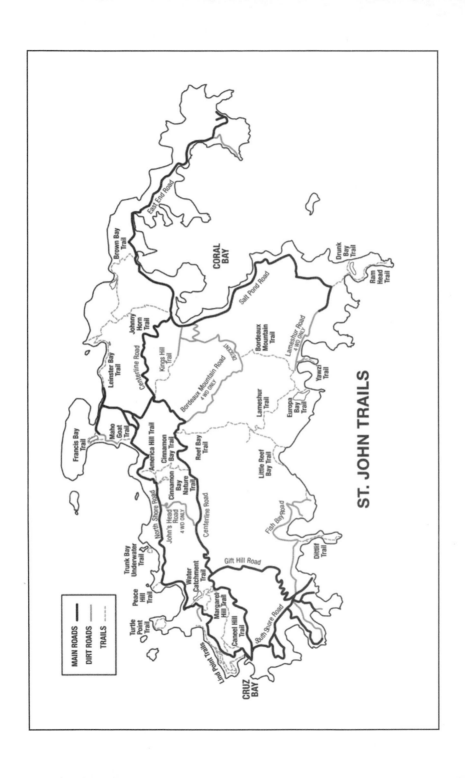

ST. JOHN TRAILS

MAIN ROADS ——
DIRT ROADS ·········
TRAILS -----

CRUZ BAY

CORAL BAY

East End Road

Brown Bay Trail

Drunk Bay Trail

Ram Head Trail

Salt Pond Road

Johnny Horn Trail

Bordeaux Mountain Trail

Lameshur Road 4 WD ONLY

Centerline Road

Kings Hill Trail

Bordeaux Mountain Road 4 WD ONLY

Yawzi Trail

Leinster Bay Trail

Lameshur Trail

Europa Bay Trail

Francis Bay Trail

Maho Goat Trail

America Hill Trail

Cinnamon Bay Trail

Reef Bay Trail

Little Reef Bay Trail

Cinnamon Bay Nature Trail

North Shore Road

John's Head Road 4 WD ONLY

Centerline Road

Fish Bay Road

Dittlif Trail

Trunk Bay Underwater Trail

Water Catchment Trail

Gift Hill Road

Peace Hill Trail

Margaret Hill Trail

Turtle Point Trail

Caneel Hill Trail

South Shore Road

Lind Point Trails

# OFF-THE-TRAIL HIKES

Now that enough people are hiking the National Park trails to keep them well maintained, some people consider these hikes too tame. They want more of a challenge. But in most areas of St. John, thick, tangled, and thorny vegetation effectively prevents you from wandering off the trails. The only exceptions are: along the coast, where waves, cliffs, and rocks keep the vegetation away, or in the guts (river beds that are usually dry) where the occasional flow of water keeps the vegetation thinner. Hiking/scrambling in these areas will provide many hours of adventurous exploring.

All of these hikes are completely unofficial. A few are easy, with the biggest problem being the trail may be a little overgrown. Many of these hikes require rock- and/or cliff-climbing skills over slippery rocks. Sometimes the only route involves swimming and getting your daypack full of expensive gear soaking wet. One of these hikes does not have a trail at all – a machete would be helpful. There is no guarantee that you can successfully make it to the end of the trail; you may need to turn back. You can get hurt, you can get lost and no one is going to be around to help you out. Please use tons of common sense, bring plenty of water and food, and use the Trails Illustrated Topo map of St. John. Always tell someone where you are going and when to start getting worried. These hikes should be wonderful, challenging, terrific adventures, not complete disasters because you overestimated your abilities and got into trouble.

## PERKINS CAY

Degree of difficulty: easy. Time required: 15 minutes. From the Peace Hill trail, look for a trail off to the right. This leads down to Denis Bay Beach right in front of Perkins Cay. Snorkeling is excellent around the cay. You can stroll along the entire length of the beach but do not trespass on the private property at the far end.

## NON-EXISTENT ROUTE 204

Degree of difficulty: easy. Time required: 1 hour each way. Find the dirt road on the left just past Paradise Lumber on Centerline Road. Walk along the dirt road admiring the majestic views of the North Shore. Keep track of how far out of the way the road is by using the bays below: you will go from Gibney's Beach all the way over to Cinnamon Bay before swinging back the other way. After passing a few villas, the road turns into a terrible donkey track and eventually descends to the North Shore Road very close to the Peace Hill parking area. Return to Centerline using the Water Catchment Trail to make a nice loop.

## BROWN BAY COASTAL HIKE

Degree of difficulty: moderate. Time required: 3 hours each way. From Brown Bay Beach continue following the coastline past the ruins and around the point, along a series of rocky beaches to end up at Waterlemon Cay Beach. Walking is easy on the beaches, but there are a few spots where you must scramble up and over the large boulders. Be prepared to get your feet wet. If it is not too rough, snorkeling is good at the different fringing reefs that parallel the shore (watch out for urchins). All of the clothing scattered around is from illegal aliens swimming to shore. On the last really long beach, see if you can spot the wonderful cluster of rocks that gives the area its name: **Threadneedle Point.** Theses beaches are the closest point on St. John to Tortola – there used to be an occasional swimming race but it has not happened in a very long time now.

## COCOLOBA COASTAL HIKE

Degree of difficulty: easy then increasingly difficult. Time required: 1/2 hour each way to beach, much longer to keep going. From the Fish Bay Road, take your first right turn and go past the Guavaberry Nursery, then continue up and over the steep hill (you will need four-wheel drive to do it). Park along the road before it turns to the right onto private property (the owner is really sick of people parking on his land and is threatening to put a chain across the road way before the steep hill). Walk down towards the dock and take the trail to the left through the mangroves to the coast. Continue along the coast to the left past the shallow bay to a secluded sandy Cocoloba Beach. This is not a great place to swim because of urchins, very shallow water, waves, and strong current. In order to continue further along the coast, you will need to be a good rock scrambler. The going is not too bad all the way past the next little sand beach and around the point to the Reef Bay side. But from here, it is very, very difficult and dangerous. The sensible thing to do is go back the way you came.

## FISH BAY GUT AND BATTERY GUT

Degree of difficulty: very difficult. Time required: 3 to 5 hours each way. To complete either trail requires serious rock climbing skills. From the Fish Bay Bridge, follow the gut (riverbed) uphill, scrambling over the boulders and walking in the water. There are many pools of fresh water along the way full of crayfish, crabs, snails, and fish. Locals enjoy swimming in them. After about ½ hour you will come to some very large cliffs and the intersection of the two guts: Battery Gut to the left and Fish Bay Gut to the right. Fish Bay Gut is easier, but still requires a great deal of expertise in rock scrambling. After a few hours of hard work, this gut will become quite small and you will be able to spot a dirt road alongside it. Follow that road (L'Esperance Road) uphill to where it comes out on Centerline Road, between John's Head Road and the Centerline Overlook.

The Battery Gut requires excellent rock-scrambling skills and serious cliff-climbing skills. There is a 70-foot waterfall cliff that must be negotiated – it is slippery and dangerous. Above the waterfall, the gut eventually leads behind Pine Peace School, along a residential area then past the Majestic Concrete Plant (that is where the gray muck is coming from) to end up on Centerline Road at the beginning of the Catherineberg straight away.

## L'ESPERANCE ROAD

Degree of difficulty: hard. Time required: 2 hours one-way. From Centerline Road, a few curves after John's Head Road, find the dirt road on the right with a large gate. Park here and start walking downhill, following the old plantation road. You will come to a large number of mango trees and the beginning of the Fish Bay Gut on the right side. There are ruins along the way that you may be able to find in the bushes, one of the easiest spots is at the bottom on the long downhill stretch just before it starts climbing again. There are ruins to the right and way in the bush to the left (I got to see a mother bat nursing her baby in one of these buildings!).

The road then climbs up to a grassy area – there is a Trail Bandit trail off to the right that leads to a magnificent Baobab tree and continues on into Fish Bay. A little further on and you will be able to see the water at Reef Bay. Continue down the hill (perfectly sloped at 7 degrees so the oxen could haul heavy carts up this hill) until the road ends.

Fortunately, the Trail Bandit has been here and now instead of having to fight your way through terrible thorny brush, you can just follow the trail down to either the Reef Bay Trail (to the left) or to Little Reef Bay Beach to the right. (Please check Update Chapter for more L'Esperance info)

## EAST END BAY

Degree of difficulty: very difficult, time required: 1 ½ hours each way.
A developer has paved roads into this area, but no one is allowed to use them. So this is still the only way to get to the other beach. This walk requires very good rock-climbing skills. From Privateer Beach, follow the coastline to the left. You will have to wade in waist-deep water to get by some of the boulders (short people may need to swim). Continue along the coast until you get to a small rocky beach. Look for the rappelling rope on the left hand side of the beach. Use the rope to walk straight up the cliff – be careful of the loose rubble underfoot. The rope is a nasty one that rips up your hands but it is the only way up the cliff.

Once on top follow the path over the top of the hill and down the other side to a small rocky beach. This is a lee shore which makes for spectacular beachcombing on this beach and the main beach over to the left (which I call Basketball Beach since the time I found a brand new basketball <u>and</u> a daypack to carry it in on this beach. I took it to my friend Al who had discovered that building a basketball court on a cliff meant he needed to buy balls by the dozens). If it is not too rough, the snorkeling here is pretty good. Now that the new road is causing storm water erosion and dumping silt into the bay, we will see how the reef holds up.

## COASTAL EXPLORATIONS

Degree of difficulty: very difficult. Time required: Start early in the morning, it may take all day. If you like exploring the coastline in between beaches, St. John offers plenty of routes to try (make sure you choose a calm day – those points are very dangerous when the waves are crashing). Only a few can be walked and scrambled without you being forced by cliffs to actually swim rather than just wade in shallow water. Some mostly-dry routes to try are: Cruz Bay to Salomon, Drunk Bay to Concordia, and Johnson Bay to Friis Bay.

Most of the routes between beaches are easier to traverse via the water rather than by land (assuming you are a really good long-distance snorkeler). But that creates a problem – how to carry water and food, and how to get back. If you have someone meet you at the next beach it will solve both problems. Otherwise you will need to swim back the way you came and either figure out how to carry water with you (mesh bags tow nicely), or stick to the few routes with facilities at one end and bring money. These routes are: Maho Beach to Cinnamon Bay Beach, Cinnamon Bay to Peter Bay then around to Trunk Bay, Perkins Cay to Jumbie Beach then on to Trunk Bay, and Frank Bay to Gallows Point. These are long snorkels and feel even longer on the way back when you are tired. Make sure you have serious sun protection and judge your stamina wisely. I recommend a nice long rest and then a chocolate ice cream bar for an energy boost before swimming back.

# JEEP TOURS

The very best way to see St. John is to rent a jeep. There is so much more to the island than Trunk Bay and the only real way to explore is by having your own wheels.

## DRIVING: THE WAY WE DO IT HERE

To some people, just driving on St. John is quite an adventure because we do things a little different here. (Please check the Update chapter for additional information on GPS and Google Maps).

We drive on the left side (which confuses everyone except the British and Japanese) but we use cars built for driving on the right (thereby confusing everyone and causing dazzling night blindness because the oncoming headlights are angled right at you).

The best explanation for why we drive on the left that I've heard is: since we have narrow, winding, cliff-hugging roads, it is important for our drivers to know exactly where the cliff drops off. With the driver seated on the left side and the car driving on the left side – it is easy to stick your head out the window to see exactly how close your wheels are to falling off the cliff.

It shouldn't take you long to get the hang of driving on the "wrong" side. Your rental car might have an arrow to remind you which way left is. If not, ask your passengers to help you remember – especially at intersections. This is the easiest time to get confused (good thing we only have a few intersections).

Driving on the left also puts us in an excellent position to talk to our friends walking on that side of the road. Of course, we also like to stop to chat with our friends on the right side of the road. Sometimes we hold up traffic, but please don't get upset with us over this. Socializing is very important on St. John, and being in too much of a hurry to stop and chat is considered rude. Simply wait until it's clear, then go around.

One of the first things you'll notice is that all the roads are steep and curvy (Centerline Road has 159 curves in the 7 ½ miles from Cruz Bay to Coral Bay). The official speed limit is 10 miles per hour in the city (Cruz Bay) and 20 miles per hour in the country (everywhere else). These low speed limits are not a big problem because it is very hard to go any faster while staying on the road. You will never make it to fourth gear – forget about overdrive.

Because of all the curves and hills, it is very difficult to find a safe place to pass. This will not prevent locals from passing anyway, which can get pretty exciting. We have all driven these roads thousands of times so we are not just admiring the view. Sometimes we are late for work and in a hurry. The safest and most polite thing for you to do is to get the heck out of our way.

When you see someone behind you, pull over if possible or just slow way down when you get to a straightish stretch and wave them by with your hand. We use hand signals a lot because not everyone's car electrical system is in working order (some people even have jeeps so old that they never came equipped with turn signals) or just to emphasize the next move, or especially because we like to wave at each other.

We also give our horns a workout. When you are heading around a sharp turn, beep, so the person coming the other way will know you're there. If you hear a beep (a good rule of horns is the deeper the beep the bigger the truck), slow down and wait for the other car to appear. The large trucks and taxis cannot make it around some of the curves without taking up both lanes, so be prepared to give them room.

Almost all of our vehicles are four-wheel drive. As soon as you see some of our 35-degree hills, you'll know why. According to U.S. highway engineers any incline more than 7 ½ degrees is considered too steep. They obviously did not lay out St. John's roads. It may look like Mount Everest, but your jeep has already climbed it many times – it is possible.

Just put yourself in first gear (automatics use 2ND or LOW gear), tell the folks in the back to hang on, and go for it. If a large, slow truck or a wheezing "island car" is going up in front of you, wait at the bottom until you are sure they are going to make it, then you go. Going downhill works the same way: shift into a lower gear so that the transmission will help slow you down, then pump your brakes to remain at a steady, controlled speed. If it has been raining, even just a little, the roads are going to be extremely slippery – you may need four-wheel drive even on the easy hills.

There are a few unpaved roads that I identify as really requiring four-wheel drive expertise and your jeep may *not* have ever done these successfully. Don't ruin your vacation by overestimating your ability.

Goats, donkeys, cows, pigs, chickens (and people) all have the right of way. St. John cows have learned that they cause more damage to vehicles than vehicles do to them so they are not intimidated at all. The cows do not budge. Even when you nudge them with the bumper they don't move. This important cow information is passed down to each generation, Darwin's survival of the fittest at work. Goats, pigs, donkeys, dogs, chickens, cyclists and joggers are aware that they won't win in a collision with a car, so they will at least try to get out of your way unless they are in a big enough herd to feel invincible.

Are you scared yet? Don't be. Since everyone is going fairly slowly, and we all know every inch of these roads, it is very easy to avoid "mash-ups" (accidents) by paying attention and dodging taxis, stopped cars, and animals. Unfortunately, this means that you, too, will have to be concentrating on driving and not on sightseeing, so either take turns being the driver or stop on the side of the road to get a good look.

As if we didn't have enough obstacles, the VI Government has decided we need speed bumps – and they pop up overnight all over the place. As long as you are not driving too fast, it shouldn't be too terrible if you get surprised by one – your passengers may hit their head on the roof, but the front end of your car shouldn't fall off. This will not be true if you are speeding.

Of course, the Virgin Islands Government has some things to say about driving. You must wear a seatbelt at all times. This applies to drivers and front-seat passengers, and babies must be in a proper car seat. Passengers in the back seat, in the back of pick-up trucks or in taxis do not have to be belted (I know it doesn't make a lot of sense since those are the ones most likely to fall out, but that's the law). This is a fairly new law (1991) and the police department loves enforcing it with $50.00 tickets, so buckle up.

At the time of this writing, it is still technically legal to drink while driving. (However, there is pending legislation to outlaw this dangerous practice.) Being drunk while driving is clearly illegal. Remember: our roads are difficult even when sober. If you have had anything alcoholic to drink, let someone else drive.

A U.S. driver's license can be used for up to three months and other countries driver's licenses are acceptable even without an International Driver's License.

The **Official Virgin Islands Drivers Manual** is an extremely interesting booklet, (unfortunately very hard to get a hold of) which lists all the laws pertaining to driving, as well as other helpful information. For example:

Title 20, Section 492 of the VI Code states that it is illegal to:

a) Drive on the sidewalk

b) Operate a motor vehicle without at least one hand on the steering wheel.

This book also offers medical advice: "When applying a tourniquet in order to stop serious bleeding, the best thing to use in case of emergency is a neck tie."

And mechanical advice: "In case the carburetor of the vehicle is on fire, you should smother said fire with cloth or dirt. In case of an electrical short: if the short is causing the wires of your vehicle to smoke, you should disconnect the battery terminal."

My advice for emergencies is: if your car breaks down, or you need help, first try calling the car rental folks if your cell phone works. If you don't have reception, just flag down the next car, and ask them to help you out.

# JEEP TOUR PICK LIST

With a rental jeep, the whole island is open to explore. Each of the jeep tours identifies all the beaches, trails, overlooks, and historic sights along the way with exact locations and lots of information about each one.

## TOUR #1 - The Big Loop
The Big Loop starts in Cruz Bay then covers the North Shore Road, Centerline Road, Gift Hill Road, and South Shore Road. The Big Loop tour can be done many times – each day pick another trail to hike, a different beach to try, and a different ruin to visit. If you only have time to do one trip, this is the one.

The basic St. John trip is: take the North Shore Road, stopping at the overlooks, then Trunk Bay for sunbathing and snorkel time, and on to Annaberg for a tour of St. John history. Return along Centerline Road, going straight back to town, or if there's time, take Gift Hill Road to South Shore Road and back to Cruz Bay.

## TOUR #2 - Centerline-Coral Bay-Salt Pond-Lameshur
This trip takes you across the island to see the "other side" of St. John. If you can't snorkel the North Shore because of northern swells, it will be calm at Salt Pond. It takes about 1 hour to get from Cruz Bay to Salt Pond, so it's possible to do this in half a day. However, there is so much to do at Salt Pond and Lameshur that it's better to make a full day of it. Why not stop for dinner at one of the restaurants in Coral Bay on the way back?

The road to Lameshur Bay definitely requires four-wheel drive and many rental companies prefer that you don't take their cars to Lameshur. It is possible to walk the last part of the road to the beach (about 1 mile over a hot, steep hill).

## TOUR #3 - Coral Bay, East End
This East End Trip takes you to see Coral Bay, and then out to the even more isolated East End. There are no National Park beaches out here, just little bays that you might want to try snorkeling, the trailheads for Brown Bay and Johnny Horn Trails, and some ruins at Hermitage.

## TOUR #4 - Fish Bay Road
Fish Bay is not part of the National Park and it is now mostly paved. However, it does have a nice hike out to Dittlif Point where there are a couple of snorkel spots, and it takes you through the different sections of the Fish Bay subdivision over to Parret Bay Beach.

## TOUR #5 - Bordeaux Mountain Road
This partially-paved road leads through the lush tropical forest along the crest of the highest mountain on St. John. But then comes a very, very difficult (most times impossible) four-wheel drive descent to Coral Bay (see "Update chapter for more information on Bordeaux Mountain Road).

**TOUR #6 - Cruz Bay "Back Side" Loop**

This short loop starts and ends in Cruz Bay, going around the "back side" of town along Enighed Pond, past Turner Bay, Frank Bay, Gallows Point and back to town along Cruz Bay Beach. It makes a nice hike except for one killer hill.

**TOUR # 7 – "Extras": Maria Bluff and Contant Loops**

These two short loops offer great views (like every road on St. John), but not much else. If you are having fun driving your jeep and have been everywhere else, or if you want to see more of the residential areas of the island, go for it.

## JEEP TOURS IN DETAIL

# TOUR # 1: THE BIG LOOP
# NORTH SHORE / CENTERLINE / GIFT HILL
# AND SOUTH SHORE ROADS

Most of the perfect white sandy beaches, the historic ruins, and trails in the National Park can be found on the North Shore Road. If you only have time for one trip, this is the one to do. There are so many things to see on this tour that it takes three maps to show them all. The first on page 109 shows the North Shore Road from Cruz Bay to Trunk Bay. The second on page 110 shows from Cinnamon Bay to Annaberg then Centerline to John's Head Road. The third on page 111 shows the rest of Centerline, and all of Gift Hill Road and South Shore Road.

### CRUZ BAY - NATIONAL PARK VISITORS CENTER

From Cruz Bay, follow the waterfront past **Nature's Nook** (a good place to stop and get cold drinks, fruits, vegetables and snacks). On the left is a small parking lot usually full of taxis, which is supposed to be used by visitors going to the National Park Visitors Center. If you can't find a parking place, go on a little further, past the baseball field to the next left, and follow this road around to the back of the National Park building.

The Park employees are very comfortable in their new, enormous, expensive building – too bad the Park was not as concerned about the visitor's comfort. Millions of taxpayer dollars were spent but there are no bathroom facilities for visitors in the new building. Instead, you get to use the horrible, antiquated, usually broken old toilet houses. These facilities are supposed to be open every day from 8:00 to 4:30, but frequently are closed. Do not count on them being available.

The National Park Visitors Center is suppose to be getting some new displays but so far only has the very nice, large, 3-dimensional model showing off all the hills and valleys of St. John. A ranger is on duty to answer questions and can tell you about any special hikes and other programs scheduled during your stay. Check the Annaberg schedule – it is much nicer to tour the ruins when the rangers are out there, which is not everyday. If there are not going to be any rangers, get a self-guiding Annaberg brochure.

Be sure to ask for the best publication that the Park produces (sometimes they forget to put enough out in the rack) – the **free VI National Park Brochure** called *A Treasure Trove of Discoveries*. It has a decent map (only two imaginary roads are shown), lots of general information, and an excellent picture above and below the waterline showing 47 things that you should be able to easily see during a week's stay on St. John.

Other attractions at the Visitors Center are: a super selection of books for sale on fish, birds, animals, history, (all sold at the actual book list price which is unusual around here), a park newspaper, and different brochures about the park. Anyone planning to do serious hiking should invest in the *Trail Illustrated Topo Map of St. John* (waterproof, very accurate, terrific for seeing the mountainous terrain).

## LIND POINT TRAIL

From the National Park Headquarters, there is a nice, easy, well-maintained trail to the Lind Point Overlook, Salomon Beach, Honeymoon Beach, and Caneel Bay Beach. The Lind Point Trail is the only way to get to Salomon and Honeymoon beaches. It takes about 25 minutes to get to Salomon, another 10 minutes to get to Honeymoon, then another 10 minutes to get to Caneel. (For trail details see page 69, for beach details see page 38.)

## SET MILEAGE TO ZERO

When you are finished at the Park Headquarters, follow the road going out of town. In order to match the mileage marks given in this book, set your trip mileage to zero where the pavement changes at the edge of town from concrete to blacktop. This is right at the end of the Mongoose Junction buildings. The reason why the road has two different surfaces is because all roads in the National Park are maintained with Federal Funds, and usually kept in excellent condition by a private company. All the other roads are maintained by the Virgin Islands Government's Public Works Department and St. John Roads are often at the bottom of the funding priority list.

## CANEEL HILL AND MARGARET TRAILS

Just past the Mongoose Junction complex on the right, hidden in the bushes, is the beginning of the Caneel Hill Trail and the Margaret Hill Trail. Both are very steep difficult hikes, one goes to the North Shore Road (60 minutes), the other to Centerline Road (90 minutes). (See page 69 for details.)

## CRUZ BAY OVERLOOK

Start up the hill, and where the road curves to the right, there is a lookout area (0.2 mi) on the left. Stop here for an excellent view of Cruz Bay. The island to the right that most of the ferries are coming from and going to, is **St. Thomas.** The little island just outside of the bay is **Steven's Cay.** No one lives there and it is difficult to land a boat on the rocky shore, but the far side has an excellent reef that is used frequently as a dive site when the current is not too strong.

Just below you, that first section of the bay is known as the **Creek.** It used to be where the barges arrived but they have now moved to the Enighed Pond Cargo Port which is past the school. Everything we need comes to St. John by water, on the barges. Gasoline, sand, gravel, cement, wood, food, water – everything comes by boat. Our prices are high because most of our goods start in Miami, get shipped to St. Thomas, trucked across St. Thomas to Red Hook, then loaded onto the barge, then offloaded in St. John and trucked to the store. Lots of middlemen, shippers, and tax collectors along the way, all adding to the cost of the product. For fruit and vegetables coming from Miami, the shipping cost can be equal to the cost of the food (a dollar's worth of tomatoes can cost a dollar to ship).

The white building on the water's edge of the Creek is the **U.S. Customs House** and the offices for the **Tortola ferries.** Like everything else, the only way for a sick person to get to the St. Thomas hospital is to go by boat. St. John's hospital boat, the *Star of Life,* is berthed just to the left of the Customs building.

The saga of the hospital boat is: a few years ago, St. John was in dire need of a boat because the old one was constantly broken down. The government officials who went shopping to replace it somehow ended up with a plug (the form built to make a mold) that never worked properly, barely floated, and cost far, far more than the budgeted amount. That boat is still sitting in dry dock in St. Thomas, running up an incredible daily storage fee bill, while everyone tries to lay the blame on someone else. (This has been going on for over five years now.)

When St. John was forced to use ferries to transport patients, the drug enforcement officials came up with a drug runner's boat that was confiscated during a big bust. This boat was outfitted to transport stretchers, given to St. John and is the one currently in use.

The very frustrated EMT's and *Star of Life* crewmembers have set up a non-profit organization to collect donations needed to keep the ambulance boat running whenever the VI Government cannot find the funds to do so (a very frequent occurrence).

The red-roofed building on the peninsula is the **Battery.** This building was part of the island defense system long ago, and has been used in many ways by the government since. Currently, it is the residence for the Administrator of St. John and contains the offices of a few government agencies.

The cluster of gray buildings on the peninsula to the right is **Gallows Point,** a hotel/condominium complex (yes, the hanging gallows used to be there and the cemetery is conveniently right next door). To the left of Gallows is **Lavender Hill** – luxury condos, and then further to the left is the never ending construction mess of one of our new monstrous developments **Grande Bay.**

The large yellow building to the left is **Julius Sprauve School,** one of two public schools on the island. Both are elementary schools through the ninth grade – high school students must take the ferry to St. Thomas.

Above the town is the new development that currently wins my award (heavily contested by too many candidates) for making the biggest disaster area – **Serenusa,** commonly referred to as Sera-Nuisance.

### BIOSPHERE RESERVE FACILITY/TWO SHORTCUTS

Back on the road, on the left is **Asolare** (an expensive restaurant with a great view to match the great food), **Estate Lindholm** (a bed and breakfast), and at the top of the hill (0.3 mi) is the housing for National Park employees.

The turnoff leads to the **Biosphere Reserve facility,** where botanists, marine biologists and other scientists conduct research studies. Also at the entrance to the housing area is a marked "spur" trail (shortcut) going down .4 miles to intersect with the Lind Point Trail (go left to Salomon, right to Honeymoon). On the right side of the main road is another shortcut to the Caneel Hill and Margaret Hills Trails. There is no real reason to go to the Biosphere: there is no visitor info or displays and the unofficial trail to the beaches that started between the buildings no longer exists.

Continuing on, you are now on the North side of St. John. The North Shore is almost entirely National Park land, which means this series of beautiful bays and perfect white sandy beaches, surrounded by forests stretching up to the tops of the mountains, is undisturbed by many buildings or houses. Note: Any roads not mentioned are private driveways; please do not go down them.

## CANEEL OVERLOOK

After a few curves, there is an overlook where you can pull over to get a good look at the scenery (0.9 mi). Down and to the right, that entire large peninsula is the **Caneel Bay Resort.** It has seven beaches (a different one for each day of your week's vacation), tennis courts, swimming pool, and, no, that's not a golf course – it's just a lawn.

Mr. Rockefeller, who purchased much of St. John back in the 1950's, obviously saved the best for his hotel. This is it. Even though he doesn't own the resort any more, his rules are still followed – no high rises and all the buildings must blend in so that they cannot be seen from this overlook.

All landscaping is "natural" and the resident botanist and staff work hard to keep it that way (compare this landscaping to the Westin's tropical-movie-set look).

Caneel was badly flooded and wind-damaged by Hurricane Hugo. All the huge palm trees were lost, but luckily, Mr. Rockefeller had insured the palm trees with Lloyd's of London (who would ever think of insuring trees?). So about a month after the storm, while we were still waiting for electricity to be restored, a barge pulled into Cruz Bay full of huge, mature palm trees (where do you buy these?) that were loaded on to a truck, taken to Caneel and planted. Hurricane Marilyn also damaged trees and once again they were replaced – these folks have got great insurance!

With all that prime, flat land, Caneel Bay was one of the first sugar plantations to be established on St. John. Fortunately, the ruins left from that era are considered an asset to the resort and were not destroyed during the construction. The well-maintained sugar factory ruins can be visited, and the old horse mill has been converted into a restaurant; it's the building with the round roof.

Looking over the peninsula, the large island is **Jost Van Dyke,** one of the British Virgin Islands. To visit the BVI's you need a passport or proof of citizenship, because it is a different country. Ferries leave St. John regularly to go to **Tortola** and Jost Van Dyke; you may see one of them from here (easy to spot because they usually leave great clouds of black smoke behind them). **Henley Cay** is the small island between the peninsula and the larger island behind it (Lovango). Henley Cay used to be a fishing camp for jet setters back in the fifties who arrived by boat from Puerto Rico. The camp is now abandoned.

If you have a boat to get there, this Cay is great fun to explore. Go to the right from the beach, past the camp ruins (uncovered cistern has water and a tap, but also contains years of leaves and crud so don't drink it) and hike around the shoreline. The rock pools are excellent, but snorkeling on the weather side is tricky due to strong currents and waves.

Behind Henley is **Lovango Cay,** which is the last in a chain of Cays going over to St. Thomas. You may not be able to see them all from here but their names in order are Lovango, Mingo, Grass and Thatch Cays then St. Thomas. Only Lovango is inhabited, the handful of folks living here commute to St. John in dinghies. (The story of how Lovango got its name: as the location of a brothel during the pirate days, it was where you "Love and Go".)

It's hard to tell, but there is another cay just behind Lovango, **Congo Cay,** the narrow passage between those two offers great snorkeling, (many of the day sail boats go there for the snorkeling stop) and at the eastern end of Congo are **Carval Rocks,** a super scuba dive spot.

## CANEEL ENTRANCE

After a few more curves and hills you come to the entrance to Caneel Bay (1.3 mi). On the opposite side of the road is the trailhead for hiking back to Cruz Bay (Margaret Hill Trail) or to Centerline Road (Water Catchment Trail). The park has a sign showing which trail goes where that is mostly accurate.

## CANEEL BAY RESORT

Turn onto the Caneel Resort road. Currently the gate area is a construction site, mandated by Homeland Security to be capable of repelling armed terrorists (the foundation goes down about 10 feet!). Caneel no longer welcomes visitors (please see the Update chapter for more information about Caneel). If you are willing to pay the outrageous $20 fee to enter the resort, you will be directed to take the second left to the visitor's parking lot and follow the path down the hill. To get to Caneel Bay Beach, take the path past the gift shop (clothes, U.S. newspapers, books, cold drinks, and gifts), and keep going straight in between the front desk building and the outdoor bar. Notice the beautiful tropical flowers and plants along the way. If you want to hike the Turtle Point Trail, Caneel will tell you that it is not allowed. In the past you just went to the little shelter to wait for the shuttle bus and asked to be dropped off at the trail. (For beach details see page 38, for trail details see page 65)

From the Caneel entrance, the road climbs again. On the right is the turnoff for the dirt road leading to the water catchment basin (1.6 mi). Before Caneel got a reverse osmosis plant (converts seawater to drinking water) this is how they caught and stored their water.

It seems silly that no one is using it today, since the rest of the island still has a severe water shortage problem and all the workings are still in place.

It's probably yet another one of those sensible ideas that are defeated by red tape and lawyers.

## HAWKSNEST BEACH

Once up and over the hill you come to Hawksnest Beach (1.8 mi). Hawksnest features the closest reef to the shore – it comes right up to the sand and is a very popular beach because it's the first one you get to driving from town. This is a beautiful, wide, long white sandy beach that is great for swimming, sunbathing, or snorkeling. (For details see page 39.)

## GIBNEY'S BEACH

Go up and over the hill from Hawksnest Beach. Don't go down the first road to the left (private driveway), but the second road to the left has a small area to park in front of the magnificent, ornate gate (2.3 mi). This gate stays closed unless someone has rented the Oppenheimer house for a party. Look for the small people-size door in the gate. The dirt road leads to Gibney's Beach (or Little Hawksnest or Oppenheimer's Beach), which is partially a National Park beach and partially not a National Park beach. This is a long sandy beach, with lots of shade trees. (For details see page 39.)

## HAWKSNEST OVERLOOK, EASTER ROCK

From Gibney's Beach, go up the hill to the next left turn at the top of the hill. Along the stone wall is a small area to pull over and admire Hawksnest Bay (2.4 mi). The large rock on the left hand side is **Easter Rock.** Legend has it that every Easter it rolls down the hill and somehow gets back up again (I checked this Easter and, well, it *did* look sort of wet).

## PEACE HILL

A little further on at the bend in the road is a small parking lot (2.6 mi) and a trail that leads to Peace Hill and the windmill ruins. The trail to Peace Hill is short (10 minutes), and leads to a spectacular view at the top of the hill. (For details see page 62.)

## NON-EXISTENT ROUTE 204

Across the road from the Peace Hill parking lot is a dirt road that, at least according to the VI Government map, is a paved two-lane road capable of taking you up to Centerline Road (Route 204). This is absolutely untrue. First it isn't paved, second it was never two lanes wide, and third, it has not been used or graded in so many years that it is now just a completely washed-out donkey trail. It is totally impassable to vehicles.

## JUMBIE BEACH

The road continues on, down the hill with an unmarked dip at the bottom that you will discover if you are going too fast, and then on the right is a small parking lot (2.7 mi). This is where to park to walk down the trail to small, sandy Jumbie Beach. (For details see page 40.)

## TRUNK BAY OVERLOOK

A little further on is the Trunk Bay overlook (3.0 mi). Stop to take a picture of one of the ten most beautiful beaches in the world (according to National Geographic).

Also if you had the miserable misfortune to see the utterly awful movie *Christopher Columbus – The Discovery,* you'll recognize this bay as where Chris was supposed to have first landed in the new world with the Nina, Pinta, and the Santa Maria.

In reality, Chris never did land on St. John, nor were there any palm trees on the island back then. But that didn't seem to bother the movie folks.

## TRUNK BAY BEACH

The next stop is Trunk Bay Beach (3.2 mi), the showpiece of the National Park beaches and host to a large volume of visitors. It also has an **underwater snorkel trail,** with signs pointing out different types of fish and coral. This enormously long sandy beach is very popular because it is beautiful and because it has a full range of facilities and lifeguards. There is an entry fee to visit during business hours, but no fee if you come really early or after 4:00. (For details see page 40.)

Leaving Trunk Bay, you come to your first serious driving challenge – **Honky Hill.** This is a very steep hill with severe switchbacks and lots of taxi traffic. When you get to a corner, honk your horn (now do you understand the name?) so that someone coming down will hear it and give you room. Take your time and use first gear. Your jeep has done this before even if you haven't. If it's wet, use four-wheel drive. At the top of the hill to the left is a very fancy gate that is the entrance to **Estate Peter Bay** (3.5 mi). This is a very exclusive subdivision. If you are interested in buying land contact a realtor, otherwise don't go down this road. It's private. (The owner maintains that Peter Bay Beach is surrounded by private property and that there is no traditional land access to it.) Peter Bay has now expanded to the other side of the road too (where do all these millionaires come from?). To keep the view pristine, power lines on the North Shore Road have always been hidden 20 feet into the bushes. The phone and power repair guys hate this and have tried repeatedly to get the poles moved to the roadside, but it was always decided that keeping the vista beautiful was worth a little inconvenience. Except for the Peter Bay folks who decided it was more important to sell a few extra lots than to keep the North Shore pretty, so they moved the poles and now ugly wires crisscross the road. Thank goodness all of the widely inappropriate Greek statues have been removed from their niches on the Upper Peter Bay wall. Perhaps someday they fill these holes with some nice, tropical, islandy artwork.

## JOHN'S HEAD ROAD

On the main road again, to the right is a dirt road called John's Head Road, which goes up to Centerline Road (3.9 mi).

Once again, the official VI Government Road Map shows this as a paved road

(Route 206) which, as you can see, is a huge exaggeration.

There were plans to pave it in 1993, but the VI Government went broke. Some of the worse curves have been concreted, but it still is a difficult road to use and definitely requires four-wheel drive. It does make a very good hiking trail.

## CINNAMON BAY

At the bottom of the hill and just on the curve where you can't see it before you've passed it, is the entrance to **Cinnamon Bay Campground** (4.2 mi). Follow the horseshoe shaped driveway around, past the taxis, and on the left is the parking lot. (Note: even entering parking lots you have to stay on the left side).

Cinnamon Bay has a huge wide beach and a little island offshore (just like Trunk Bay but further out). The campgrounds offer everything that an adventuresome visitor might need for a weeklong stay.

During high season, there may be someone providing tourist information about the various National Park programs (same info as the National Park Visitors Center gives you). The National Park Rangers hold regular evening programs on different topics at the outdoor theater just past the parking lot and sometimes there are plays or other special events. All of these programs are free so why not go? (For beach details see page 42.)

## CINNAMON BAY RUINS AND NATURE TRAIL

Cinnamon Bay also has some hiking trails and ruins – well worth visiting. The Cinnamon Bay Ruins are a self-guided tour, with signs explaining how the sugar mill operated. Behind the last building is the Cinnamon Bay Nature Trail. This is an easy trail (30 minutes) with signs identifying different trees and plants along the way. The plantation cemetery offers a peaceful place to rest. (For details see page 65.)

## CINNAMON BAY TRAIL AND AMERICA HILL TRAIL

Next on the North Shore Road is the beginning of the Cinnamon Bay Trail (mile point 4.3). This trail climbs steadily up the hill to Centerline Road (60 minutes). The America Hill Trail turns off from the Cinnamon Bay Trail and climbs to some ruins (30 minutes). (For details on Cinnamon Bay Trail see page 70, for details on America Hill Trail see page 65.)

## FRANCIS BAY OVERLOOK

The road starts to climb again, and just around the corner past the top of the hill is another overlook (4.8 mi). This one shows off Francis Bay.

The beach to the right is Maho Beach, the roofed tents on the point sticking out are in the Maho Bay Campground, and then further left is Francis Beach.

The far point is called **Mary's Point.** Legend has it that this is the location where the slaves leaped to their suicide after the 1733 uprising.

The little island further left is **Whistling Cay.** This was a quarantine station back in the plantation days. The ruins of the old customs building can be seen on the rocky beach. The customs guys used to blow their whistle to signal the passing ships to stop, hence the name. There is excellent snorkeling to the left of the customs building and good scuba diving on the back side of the island. (The only sensible way to get out there is by boat. You can rent a kayak from Cinnamon or Maho. Swimming across from Mary's Point is extremely dangerous because there are strong currents and high-speed ferries in the channel.)

## MAHO BAY BEACH

Continue on down the hill, around the corner, and you come to Maho Beach (5.2 mi). This is the closest beach to the road on St. John. (See Update for more information on Maho Bay beach)

The best part of the beach is at the far end, but first you pass a long building fronted by a stone wall. There are a few parking places alongside this structure. This is a community building, recently rebuilt, and a functioning outhouse. (For details see page 43.)

At the far end of the beach is the beginning of the **Maho Goat Trail** that can be used as a short cut to the Campground. (For details see page 63)

Leaving Maho Beach, the road gets a little confusing. The road splits into two one-way roads. Take the left fork (5.6 mi) and you'll soon come to an intersection with a two-way road (6.2 mi).

To continue on the North Shore Road and connect up with Centerline, you must turn right. Or, if you want to go back to the North Shore Road and the beaches, you also turn right.

If you want to keep following this book, go left. (And remember you are supposed to be driving on the left hand side of the road). Please be careful, in this entire area you will be sharing the road with joggers, walkers, and a family of deer.

## MARY POINT SCHOOL RUINS

A little further on, there is a nice little area to pull over on the right. As the sign says, here you can see the remains of a Danish cobblestone road that connected the three plantations in this area which had the highest population density on St. John at that time.

Recently, someone cleared a portion of this old road. I have no idea if it will stay cleared since this is the first time in thirteen years that it has happened. If it is overgrown you can still go poking around, be prepared for lots of pricker bushes.

Leave your jeep here, then walk down the road to the short trail to the schoolhouse ruins which leaves the road on the left just before the next intersection across from a big tree. The Mary Point School House was built in 1844 when the Danish Government declared it mandatory for both slave and free children to go to school. The St. John Historical Society did a great job restoring the schoolhouse. Be sure to look for the display showing the before and after photos.

## ANNABERG TRIANGLE

Back enroute, the road comes to a traffic triangle (6.4 mi). The right fork goes to the Annaberg ruins and Leinster Bay and Waterlemon Beach, the left goes to Maho Bay Campground and Francis Bay Beach. Since you may want to go to both places, I'll cover both routes with the mileage starting from here.

## LEFT TURN: Francis Bay and Maho Bay Campground

### MARY'S CREEK

The bay to your right is Mary's Creek which is part of Leinster Bay. This bay is very shallow. It is excellent for bone fishing, not good for swimming, and terrible for wading because there are lots of urchins. (Expert snorkelers can tour the mangrove swamp here, but it is really shallow and requires perfect body control).

One other thing: the cement strips across the road are drainage low points. They are also great places to bounce someone out of the backseat if you are going too fast.

### FRANCIS BAY TRAIL

Soon you come to a small parking area and a restored building (0.4 mi). The Francis Bay Nature trail starts here. It goes about a half mile through the forest, around the salt pond and then to the beach. (For details see page 63.)

### FRANCIS BAY BEACH

For those of you not into hiking to get to Francis Beach, there's another way. Take the dirt road on the right just past the parking area. Keep going to the end of the road, where you'll find room for cars to park and, hopefully, room to turn your car around if everybody parked considerately. Francis is a very large, long, sandy beach that is usually not crowded. (For details see page 44.)

### MAHO BAY CAMPGROUND

If you go straight at the dirt road turnoff to Francis Beach, you'll go up the hill to Maho Bay Campground (they finally put up some signs to help you find the way). It's a steep hill – put it in first and go slow and steady. If anyone is coming down the hill, there are a few places where it's wide enough to let two cars pass. At the crest of the hill (0.7 mi) there is another private road to the right marked dead end. Bear to the left and head down the hill (the road to the far left goes up to the new section of the Campground) into the campground parking lot (0.8 mi). Park here. The paved road down to the right is for deliveries only.

The staff here at Maho is extremely friendly. Most of the guests seem to be nice folks too. Since the entire facility is built on a hillside, there are plenty of stairs to climb. Anyone whose aerobic program uses a Stair Master is going to be able to skip their daily workout while visiting Maho.

From the parking lot you first come to the restaurant that serves excellent breakfasts and dinners at reasonable prices with a different theme cuisine every night. Their Happy Hour (4:30-5:30) features inexpensive drinks and free popcorn. The breathtaking view from the open air dining area is included free. On Monday nights there is a very funny and informative slide show entitled **'Introduction to St. John'** which is performed by the staff after dinner. Check at the front desk for the entertainment scheduled for the rest of the week.

Following the boardwalk downwards, the next level is the general store (cold drinks, ice cream bars, munchies, etc.) and a chalkboard listing the week's activities. The public is welcome to sign up for any of these at the **Activities Desk.** (The night snorkel is great!)

## LITTLE MAHO BEACH

At the boardwalk level, just below the store, is the front desk (if you have any questions), two public pay phones, and the activities sign-up desk. This is also where the Goat Trail from Maho Bay Beach comes out. Then it's 180 stairs down to the Little Maho beach. At the bottom you'll find a nice little sandy beach with lots of trees, sea kayak, windsurfer, sunfish, and snorkel rentals. (For beach details see page 45.)

## RIGHT TURN: Annaberg and Waterlemon

### ANNABERG ROAD

Turning right at the Annaberg Triangle, the road follows along the shoreline of Leinster Bay. On the left is a sign pointing out a **manchineel tree** (0.1 mi). These are 'our bad apples in Paradise.'

This is a *very* poisonous tree – its little crab apple looking fruit can be fatal. If you stand under it while it's raining, even the water running off its leaves can severely hurt you. Luckily, there are not very many of these trees on the island. Christopher Columbus accurately called them 'death apples' after one of his crew died from eating one.

Further down this road is the entrance to the new Annaberg parking lot (0.3 mi), where there is one fancy latrine (more can be found a little further down the road). Please feel free to adopt and take home any of the resident cats.

This parking lot is where you meet for the **National Park Seashore Walk.** This excellent program involves wading around the shallow water in your sneakers, lifting up rocks and peeking at amazing critters using a glass bottom bucket.

Park your car in the parking lot, and walk up the paved pathway to the Annaberg Ruins.

### ANNABERG RUINS

Annaberg is the well-preserved ruins of a sugar factory. There used to be a $4 entrance fee, but at the moment that has been discontinued. Ask at the Visitors Center in Cruz Bay if there are rangers giving tours or any special cultural events. If not, get the self-guiding brochure – usually there are no brochures at the actual Annaberg site.

Annaberg was still operating in the late 1800s. The remains of its windmill, one of five that were built on the island, is magnificent. The Park brochure identifies each building and how it was used in the sugar process. It also points out different fruit trees. The "balcony" area near the windmill offers a spectacular view out to seaward over to the **British Virgin Islands.** There is a sign identifying all the different islands you can see. They are a 'must-see.'

## LEINSTER BAY TRAIL

Just before you take a sharp right to go up the hill to Annaberg is the beginning of the Leinster Bay Trail (formerly a road). Erosion has created a very large ditch at the edge of the pavement – it will hurt your rental car to attempt this road – don't do it. Go back and park in the parking lot, and walk the extra 2 minutes. This trail leads to Waterlemon Beach (yet another sub-division of Leinster Bay) and the Johnny Horn Trail. The tiny beach is not very impressive, but the snorkeling is superb. (For details see page 45.)

The area behind the trees on Waterlemon Beach is also good for exploring. There is a little trail back there, paralleling the beach with another small trail branching off from it. These trails are not maintained regularly, so beware of the **Ketch-n-keep** – which is a bush/tree that has little prickers that will stop you in your tracks until you back up and get "un-Ketched." There are ruins scattered around, but don't play around the well because it might collapse on you.

There are a few buildings back there, part of the Annaberg estate after it was split up. This area was a cattle farm in the early 1900's. The way the cattle were exported was to swim them out to boats anchored in the bay and hoist them aboard. This required a diver to wrap a hoisting sling around the swimming cows – a job for which I can't imagine there were too many volunteers applying for.

## JOHNNY HORN TRAIL/BROWN BAY TRAIL

Further along the main trail starts the Johnny Horn Trail. This leads to the ruins of a Boy's Home that was used not too long ago; to the Brown Bay Trail; and to Coral Bay.

This trail is NOT maintained, but it is currently getting enough use to keep it clear and is a tough one. The Boy's Home is not too far. Just follow the trail up the hot, steep hill. Once you are on the far side, there is another small trail going off to the left before the trail starts going downhill again.

The ruins are at the very crest of the hill. This has a great a view of Drake's Passage and the British Virgin Islands. (For details of the Brown Bay Trail see page 74, for the Johnny Horn Trail see page 73.)

## FREDERIKSDAHL PLANTATION

Back in your car at the Annaberg Triangle, you should reset your trip meter to zero so it will read correctly as we continue our tour up to Centerline Road. If you are coming from Annaberg, go left. If you are coming from Francis or Maho Camp, stay straight; don't go to the left (very easy to do).

This is a two-way road here, so get over on the left. Ignore the paved road on the right a little further down (0.2 mi). That's the one-way road coming from the North Shore beaches. A little further on is a place on the right to pull off the road with nicely built low stone walls (0.3 mi). This is where you park to go see the ruins of **Frederiksdahl Plantation**.

## WINTBERG RUINS

Soon the road starts climbing and – before you're ready for it – a T-intersection pops up. This is on a fairly steep hill (0.5 mi) and requires a fast decision. It's best to decide which way you're going before you get there.

If you turn right, you are on the last leg of the one-way triangle that leads back to the North Shore beaches and back to Cruz Bay.

Along this road are the Wintberg ruins, including one of the few remaining chimneys that are still standing. (Chimneys are easy prey to erosion, hurricanes, and recycling of the rocks, bricks, and stones.)

Unfortunately, there is not a good place to pull over on this road. Also, the left side is a steep drop – so be extra careful. Be on the lookout for deer – a small herd lives in this area and likes to bound across the road right here.

This road is also the location of a classic St. John island car story. On one of my parents' many visits (they love St. John) I took them out to Maho Bay Campground for dinner. On the way home, right next to these ruins, my headlight fuse blew out. We were in total darkness, and, of course, had no spare fuse. My mother, who never exactly liked my rickety truck even in the daylight, was starting to become terrified. I got out my trusty flashlight, and sent dad ahead to lead the way by foot. We crept along behind him in my darkened truck, but it was slow going. Then a rental jeep came up behind us. It contained a very nice couple on their honeymoon. Once they were reassured that they were not being attacked on this isolated stretch of road by maniacs (the maniac part took a lot of reassuring), they agreed to act as my headlights. With my flashlight-wielding father in the back of my truck to act as our taillights, we headed off to Cruz Bay.

It was a long, long trip back to town. Various jeeps raced passed us along the way, but finally one driver realized our situation. He covered our rear for the remainder of the trip. So, nicely sandwiched between two good Samaritans, we made it back to civilization.

To this day, however, my mother refuses to get into my truck (even in daylight) without bringing at least two flashlights.

## KINGS HILL/CENTERLINE ROAD

The left turn continues up the mountain to connect with Centerline Road (route 10). That's the way I'm going, are you with me? This incline (it is steeper than it looks, so use low gears) is called King's Hill. It offers a spectacular view to everybody except the driver (because it's behind you).

At the top is another T-intersection – Centerline Road (1.2 mi). Right across the road from you is a nice little kiosk which has a small parking area. This is a good place to stop for a cold drink, smoothies, or a snack. (After years of not really having a name and just being referred to "the Colombo Yogurt stand on Centerline by the turnoff to Maho", the owners changed the Yogurt sign to read Colombo Cafe). To the left takes you to Coral Bay, to the right, back to Cruz Bay. Turn right.

The dirt road on the other side of the intersection is also Kings Hill Road – BUT – it is now only a trail, definitely not passable to cars anymore. Use it for hiking only. Follow the road down the hill onto the flats of Coral Valley. Continue straight along the road and you will reach the Salt Pond Road near Saver's Market.

# CENTERLINE ROAD

## CHATEAU BORDEAUX/BORDEAUX MOUNTAIN ROAD
Heading back towards Cruz Bay on Centerline, the road winds around a few switchbacks (notice the cotton plants next to the cliff – remnants of the plantation days), then comes to the highest point on Centerline Road. There is a magnificent view next to the Chateau Bordeaux Restaurant.  Many residents consider this the **most dramatic vista** in the entire Virgin Islands. This breathtaking view is of Coral Bay, Hurricane Hole, the East End and the British Virgin Islands (2.1 mi).

Once a month, this is the place to be at sunset – not to watch the sun go down, (wrong direction), but to watch the full moon rise from the sea and hover over Coral Harbor and Hurricane Hole.

Chateau Bordeaux Restaurant is a great place for lunch or drinks. During season it also offers amazing dinners by reservation only. Next door, you can get cold drinks, ice cream (try the mango sherbet) and souvenirs from the little shops.

The road leading up the hill is Bordeaux Mountain Road, leading to the Bordeaux Mountain Trail.

## REEF BAY TRAIL
Stay on Centerline Road and continue driving around a few more curves until you get down to the bottom of this hill where there's a small place on the right for maybe two cars to pull over and a stone wall on the left. This is the beginning of the Reef Bay Trail (2.4 mi). This is an excellent trail, leading to the Reef Bay Beach, sugar mill ruins, the Reef Bay Great House, and the petroglyphs and waterfall. The trail is about two miles long – all downhill going in and all uphill coming back. The National Park offers guided tours of this trail which returns you to Cruz Bay via boat. (For trail details see page 75.) Directly opposite the Reef Bay Trail head is the beginning of a Trail Bandit route down to Maho Bay – the Maria Hope Trail.

## CINNAMON BAY TRAIL
Back on Centerline, the road climbs. Sometimes you have to avoid rocks that have fallen from the steep cliffs on your right. Keep going until you come to a small area for cars to pull over on the left (3.3 mi) and a sign saying Cinnamon

Bay Trail to the right. This is the trail that leads to Cinnamon Bay Campground.

Some really avid campers hike from Cinnamon Bay to Reef Bay and back again in a single day. Just the *thought* makes my muscles cramp up! (For details on the Cinnamon Bay Trail, see page 70.)

## CENTERLINE OVERLOOK
Just a little further on is an overlook with a nice sign identifying all the islands you can see (3.6 mi). There are also some large majestic mango trees right along the road (but it's pretty hard to pick the fruit without going over the cliff.)

## CATHERINEBERG RUINS
Around a couple of more turns is a dirt road to the right, with a large sign saying Virgin Islands National Park (4.2 mi). This is John's Head Road – the jeep track that comes up from the North Shore Road that they were supposed to pave in 1993. Turn in here and drive just a little ways (or park at the beginning and walk) to the magnificent **Hammer Farm** windmill ruins.

Once there, go inside the building and try lying on your back to look up at the sky (or even better, the stars) framed by the windmill. These ruins were part of the Catherineberg Plantation, one of the more prosperous and fertile estates. The area past the ruins is one of the "in holdings" in the Park. The National Park owns all the land surrounding this private property where some of the island's most expensive houses are built overlooking the North Shore.

## COWS AND PIGS
Let's get back to Centerline Road. The small little white caps along the left side of the road are capped-off pump stations for a no-longer-used water pipeline into Cruz Bay.

Keep going and you'll come to our cement plant – Majestic, now closed; and then **Moses' Laundromat and Car Wash** (5.0 mi). The real name of the place is Neptune Richards (Moses' grandfather's name) but it's almost never referred to by that name. As you can see Moses is expanding, but it takes him awhile to finish things, so we'll have to wait and see what it's going to be. Mr. Moses is also the owner of a large and healthy herd of cows and pigs. They have the right-of-way, and they know it, so be prepared to stop and dodge them in this area.

The pigs have had to cope with a drastic change to their eating habits. Our public dump caught on fire in February 1992. Once the community finally forced the government into putting the fire out, it had to be closed. So these pigs lost their best food source.

One extremely clever pig, however, discovered that cows give milk, and he somehow convinced one cow to allow him to suckle. Either this pig is very old or this knowledge has been passed on to a new generation of pigs because you can still see a pig suckling on a cow in this area.

## ROUTE 204 (NOT PASSABLE)
The dirt road on the right, just past Moses' laundry is the beginning of what

was Route 204. It is no longer a road because it has not been graded or used in over 13 years. (Forget what the VI Government map says!) It is definitely not passable by vehicle, and you will get stuck if you attempt it. It does make a nice hike down to Peace Hill, but it is longer than you think. Rather than go straight down the hill, it traverses all the way over to above Cinnamon Bay before switching all the way back to get down to the North Shore Road.

### MYRAH KEATING SMITH COMMUNITY HEALTH CENTER

A little further down the road is a very large, impressive sign proclaiming the Myrah Keating Smith Community Health Center (5.2 mi). Hopefully you will have no reason to explore our health care facilities, but this is the place to come if you are sick or injured. If it is anything serious, get flown to the States pronto.

### GIFT HILL ROAD INTERSECTION

Next comes a turnoff (5.3 mi). This is Gift Hill Road (route 104). This corner is known as Public Works, because the buildings and the dump belong to the government agency called... optimistically... Public Works. To continue the tour, turn left here; to go back to Cruz Bay, go straight.

**Tony's BBQ** is the food van at the intersection – a very popular spot for food, and drink. It is also the unofficial cockfight arena – unofficial because it's illegal, so don't tell anyone.

## GIFT HILL ROAD

### TRAFFIC LIGHT

Hanging proudly on the Department of Public Works building is St. John's only traffic light. It is hanging on a building rather than on a street corner because St. John citizens protested successfully when the VI Government attempted to dump excess gear on St. John.

St. John never asked for any lights because we didn't need any. But St. Thomas decided one week before the end of the fiscal year (which applies to Federal Highway fund accountability) that St. John had to use three sets of traffic lights whether we wanted them or not, and whether they were needed or not. The entire plan was completely ridiculous: the stoplights were for a four-way intersection, but St. John does not have even one of those, never mind three; the lights have to be re-programmed after every power outage – a daily occurrence on St. John; and there is no intersection anywhere on the island with enough traffic volume to warrant a stoplight.

Some very nice person sent an anonymous fax to Connections alerting the community to the plan, and instantly St. Johnians sprang into action. It took a week of furious fighting, with calls to the Governor and Senators, faxes to newspapers, even threats of roadblocks, before St. Thomas finally gave up and left us alone. But they didn't bother to take the lights back, so the head of Public Works, Ira Wade, decided to hang one on his wall.

## THE DUMP

On the right is the entrance to the dump, but now called a transfer station. Since the fire, garbage is now being loaded into huge compactors and then trucked down into town, loaded on a barge, taken to St. Thomas, and trucked to their dump (which also catches fire regularly, but they seem to be able to put it out).

Our dump fire was another superb example of how St. Johnians come together to solve their problems.

The dump fire flared up and could not be put out by local firemen, so the government decided to just let it burn.

Normally, landfills are required to use layers of dirt in between the layers of garbage – and to use separate sections – so that there is some kind of firebreak. Apparently, however, Public Works on St. John just couldn't get hold of enough dirt to do accomplish this.

"We don't have the dirt," they said. (But, just in case some suitable dirt happened to show up unannounced one day, they kept plenty of public employees standing by to deal with it.) So the garbage just piled up.

Also federal regulations require the separating out of toxic materials that are not allowed to be dumped. But where else were they going to put them?

So everything went into the dump. Oil. Gas. Acids. Chemicals. Etc.

The authorities kept insisting that the dump fire was not toxic and that it wasn't a health hazard – but the citizens refused to listen to reason. (Many of them were too sick from the fumes to listen!)

The school in the area was closed by the dense fumes. Finally the St. John community came together in common purpose. Everyone signed petitions, wrote letters to the local and federal governments, and dashed off Letters to the Editor. We held town meetings, waved protest signs, and generally kicked up such a terrible fuss that the government was (much to its surprise) forced to put out the fire.

It was put out in September of 1992. Needless to say, this cost a small fortune. But the final 'cap' that is needed to make sure it never flares up again is still not in place over 10 years later. Why? Because the authorities say they can't find any dirt!

Back to the tour. On the left side by the dump is one of the few fresh water ponds on St. John (5.4 mi). The pigs and cows use it for bathing and drinking, so there are lots of animals crossing here.

## PINE PEACE/GIFT HILL SCHOOLS

The next landmark on the left, at the speed bump, is Pine Peace School (5.7 mi). This is a private elementary school that was organized by some parents who wanted an alternative to the education offered by the public school system. They have fundraising benefits twice a year that are great fun, and you are welcome to attend.

Further up the hill are a private junior high and high school. The names of these schools can be a problem. The area of St. John known as Pine Peace is on the South Shore Road near the E & C gas station and Pine Peace store. The elementary school was originally located there, and they kept the name despite their move. In 1995 they merged with St John's first high school which was named the Coral Bay School even though they never held a single class in Coral Bay. In fact the Coral Bay School held classes in what is known as the Lumberyard building, even though that Lumberyard went bankrupt over 15 years ago Anyway, a new, combined name was created which so far, actually matches where the campuses are located – the **St. John School on Gift Hill.** Hopefully they will not move and mess up that name.

Just past the St. John School is a very large affordable housing residential complex called **Bellevue.** It also has a Community Center where many groups hold meetings, and someday will be the home of an outdoor theater facility.

There are a number of dirt roads going off Gift Hill Road, all of which are private so you don't need to go down them unless you've been invited to someone's house.

It can be difficult on St. John to find someone's house that you've been invited to because these roads don't have any names. Just a little further on up the hill you can see how one person solved this problem. The dirt road on the right (5.9 mi), with the large blue concrete creation is known as the... come on, you've got it... the **Fork In the Road!** (Actually this fork changes colors frequently and changes shape whenever someone knocks it down – again).

## GIFT HILL

Keep going, up to the crest of Gift Hill (6.1 mi), with an altitude of 827 feet, and then downhill past the Cable TV receiver dish on the right (6.3mi). Back before Cable and Satellite TV, the top of Gift Hill was best spot for TV reception. Superbowl Sunday parties were held next to the dumpsters: portable generators ran the TV's, extra long antennae were created, everyone brought their own chair and coolers full of drinks – what fun we had!

Where the road flattens out is the main entrance for the Virgin Grand Estates (6.4 mi), another expensive, exclusive subdivision. This road eventually ends up on the South Shore Road by the Westin Vacation Club where there is a locked gate to prevent you from using this as a shortcut. (That brick road is not really brick. They have a machine that rolls over freshly-poured concrete to make the brick lines. Then it's all painted red.)

## GIFT HILL DESCENT

Continue driving up the small hill. Then start the breathtaking descent to the South Shore Road (6.6 mi). Put your car in a low gear, pump your brakes, and take your time. This is steep, but ain't the view wonderful! The bay in front of you is Rendezvous Bay, with Dittlif Point to the left and Bovocoap Point to the right.

## SOUTH SHORE ROAD / FISH BAY ROAD INTERSECTION

Once you've made it to the bottom (6.9 mi), stay on the pavement and turn right onto the South Shore Road (route 104 still). The road to the left is Fish Bay Road, which is another chapter.

# SOUTH SHORE ROAD

## BOATMAN POINT ROAD AND MONTE BAY TURNOFF

About 50 feet past the intersection is the paved Boatman Point Road on the left, which leads to the road to Monte Bay Beach. (For beach details see page 54.)

## CHOCOLATE HOLE BEACH

Go down the tight S-turns, past the speed bumps, and in a while, on the left, will be the turnoff to Chocolate Hole East (7.2 mi).

There are two beaches to choose from on this road: Chocolate Hole or Hart Bay. To get to the Chocolate Hole Beach, go straight down the road while following the massive construction site fence on the right. The enormous cactus are called **Dildo Cactus** (no, I didn't make that up). It is used by fishermen for bait in their fish traps, and it also makes excellent firewood when dry.

Keep following the fence until you get to the end – Chocolate Hole Bay (0.4 mi from the South Shore Road). There are quite a few boats anchored in this bay. The beach is good for swimming and for sea grass snorkeling.

(For details on Chocolate Hole Beach see page 54.)

## HART BAY BEACH

To get to Hart Bay Beach, take the first left turn on Chocolate Hole East Road onto Tamarind Drive (.01 mi). Keep going to the intersection of Tamarind Drive and Cactus Drive (0.4 mi), and then take the right fork. Just before you get to a small parking area, there is a sign on the right for the Hart Bay Trail. This will lead you down and around the salt pond to the rocky beach.

Hart Bay is the subsection of Rendezvous Bay most exposed to the open sea, so there are almost always waves. The waves combined with the rocks make for less- than-ideal snorkeling conditions outside the reef.

Whoever is in charge of the Hart Bay subdivision should be complimented on the new, clearly-marked trail leading to the beach. (For beach details see page 54.)

## WESTIN / GREAT CRUZ BAY BEACH

As you continue on the South Shore Road, be careful – there is a speed bump at the bottom of the hill just before the magnificent tree in the middle of the road. On your left is the entrance to the Westin Resort and the hotel, while on the right are the Westin's Vacation Villas (7.6 mi). (The hotel became the Westin just a quite few years ago. Prior to that it was the Hyatt Regency and before that it was the Virgin Grand, so you may hear locals refer to it by any of those names.)

The Westin has restaurants, a gift shop, an art gallery, a deli, and a bar by the pool that are open to the public. Everyone can use the beach. The pool and hot tub are reserved for guests only.

The Westin landscaping is worth a stroll. The grass is especially luxurious (try it with bare feet) and there are plenty of iguanas roaming around. The beach in high season is packed. The bay has poor visibility much of the time, so it is not very good for snorkeling. (For details see page 53.)

## MINI SHOPPING MALLS ON BOTH SIDES OF THE ROAD

A little ways past the Westin entrance is more speed bumps. The mini mall on the left has a few offices, our wonderful St. John vets, and Animal Care Center. If you would like to take home a unique souvenir, why not adopt a purebred St. John "dumpster" cat or "coconut" retriever? The grocery store in this mall went bankrupt and many of the space is not rented. You might think this would indicate a bad location for more tenant space, but apparently not. Just across the street someone built a brand new, even larger new mini mall that currently has only 2 tenants and the planned grocery store backed out. Who knows what will end up there.

## JACOB'S LADDER AND BACK TO TOWN

Past all the speed bumps, the road continues up the hill, and then goes very steeply back down the hill known as Jacob's Ladder, to the Pine Peace area (8.8 mi). (The hill is steep enough to have been named for climbing Jacob's ladder to heaven, but it was really named for the Jacob family that used to live at the top of the hill.) On the right is an auto parts store and Pine Peace Market.

After the speed bump comes the basketball court. (We're sorry to report that it is best to avoid this area at night, if possible. There have been a number of incidences of gangs of youths throwing rocks at strangers).

The E & C gas station, with its nice landscaping, is across the street from the basketball court (8.8 mi). Now is a good time to check your gauge.

## THE MARKETPLACE AND WAPA

Around the next curve, atop a hill to the right, is the massive, 3-storey Marketplace building. This is as close to a shopping mall as you are going to find on St. John. Tenants come and go – at the moment you can find a large, well-stocked, gourmet grocery store, a drugstore, St. John's only bookstore (with espressos, cappuccinos and lattes), the hardware store, a gym (visitors are welcome to work out), video store, and a bakery. The $3^{rd}$ floor sometimes hosts special events like plays, concerts and dance performances.

Next on the right is an orange fence (8.9 mi) enclosing the "Silver Bullet" – our generator, run by WAPA (Water and Power Authority). St. John's first generator was called the "Green Hornet," replaced by the "Silver Bullet" in the late '80s. Not too many people realize this, so many refer to it by its old name. (Many things on St. John are called what-they-used-to-be, rather than what-they-currently-are. Charming or utterly frustrating, depending on your perspective.)

Our electrical power is usually supplied from St. Thomas via an underwater cable located in Frank Bay, and the "Silver Bullet" is only fired up when St. Thomas fails us. This happens frequently. The generator is only big enough to power some of Cruz Bay; the rest of the island just gets out the candles and waits.

Both Caneel Bay and the Westin have their own generators, as do Mongoose Junction, Wharfside Village, and the Marketplace. The rest of the businesses have learned how to cope, so it won't put an end to your evening.

Across from the WAPA generator is the new sewage treatment plant on the right and a landfill area to the left with our brand new cargo port behind it. After more than 30 years, the port was finally opened (it is not yet completed).

This area used to be filled with junked cars. But then the Westin hosted a conference for governors from all over the United States, so the VI Government quickly hauled all the cars out and shipped them to St. Thomas. Thank you, governors!

## SEWAGE TREATMENT PLANT CORNER

You would think they could have found a more discreet location for the sewage treatment plant, but at least it finally got built and hopefully it is being well-run. (Maybe if they give tours it will become an asset to tourism rather than an eyesore?). Unfortunately, the plant is already at maximum capacity due to the new mega-developments that contributed not a penny to its cost, nor will they contribute to the cost of upgrading it.

This is where the road back to Cruz Bay turns to the left, because the road straight ahead is now one-way coming out of town. So turn left onto this two-way road, follow it around and then take a right at the tennis court corner. Continue up the hill, going past the WAPA standpipe, where the water trucks fill up and then over the speed hump (that is not a typo: a speed hump is wider and shorter than a speed bump – this really is a hump). Across the street from the fire station is the practice room for the **Love City Pan Dragons** – a steel pan orchestra made up of extremely talented kids. Ask when the next performance is and don't miss it. Continue up the hill to the Roundabout Intersection (9.2 mi). Go right to go back to the South Shore Road, left to go into Cruz Bay or take the right over by Dolphin Market to get onto to Centerline Road.

## ST. JOHN LIBRARY AND MUSUEM

This is the end of this tour. But the one-way system has eliminated one stop that is still worth mentioning – the St. John Library and Museum. Going back out of town from the Roundabout, just a little past **St. Ursula's Church** (notice the beautiful mosaic done by local artist Lisa Crumrine), is the dirt road on the right leading to the beautifully restored **Estate Enighed Great House** which contains the museum and library. The museum is small (but then, so is St. John) and contains some interesting exhibits and photos.

The library is upstairs from the museum. It won't let visitors check out books, but the local reference section might help you to identify a bird or fish or learn more about the history of St. John.

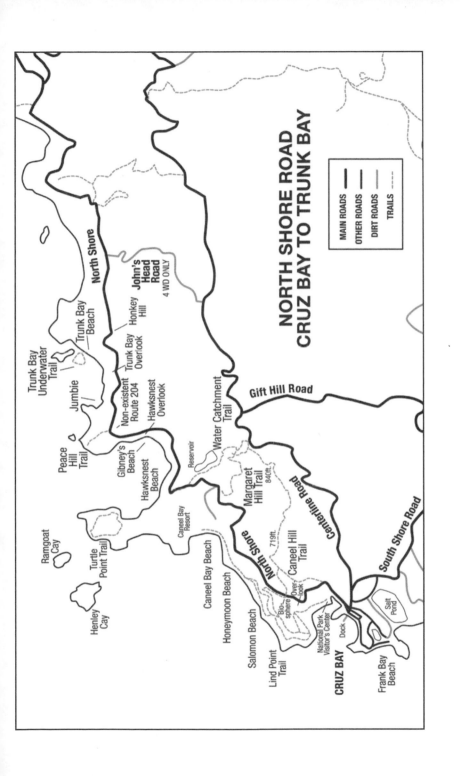

# NORTH SHORE ROAD
# CRUZ BAY TO TRUNK BAY

**MAIN ROADS** ─────
**OTHER ROADS** ─────
**DIRT ROADS** ─────
**TRAILS** ----------

**North Shore**

**John's Head Road**
4 WD ONLY

Honkey Hill

Trunk Bay Beach

Trunk Bay Overlook

Trunk Bay Underwater Trail

Jumbie

Non-existent Route 204

Hawksnest Overlook

**Gift Hill Road**

Water Catchment Trail

Peace Hill Trail

Reservoir

Gibney's Beach

Hawksnest Beach

Margaret Hill Trail
840 ft.

**Centerline Road**

Ramgoat Cay

Caneel Bay Resort

Turtle Point Trail

**North Shore**

719 ft.

Caneel Hill Trail

Henley Cay

Caneel Bay Beach

**South Shore Road**

Honeymoon Beach

Bio-sphere

Overlook

Salomon Beach

Salt Pond

Lind Point Trail

National Park Visitor's Center

Dock

**CRUZ BAY**

Frank Bay Beach

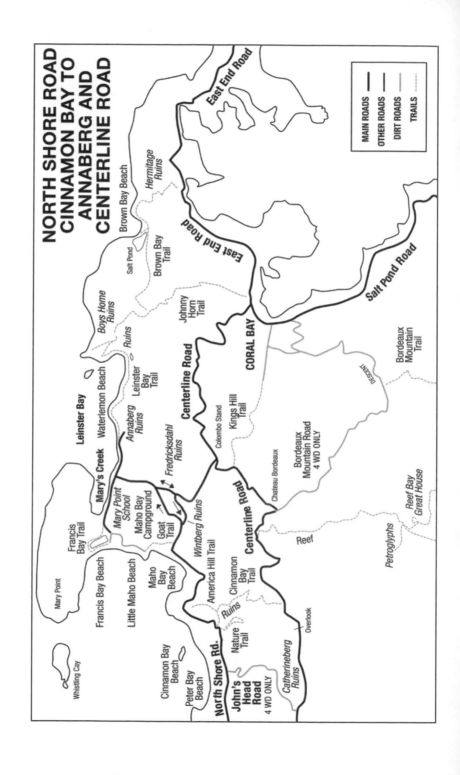

# NORTH SHORE ROAD
## CINNAMON BAY TO ANNABERG AND CENTERLINE ROAD

**MAIN ROADS**
**OTHER ROADS**
**DIRT ROADS**
**TRAILS**

East End Road

Hermitage Ruins

Brown Bay Beach

Salt Pond

Brown Bay Trail

East End Road

Salt Pond Road

Boys Home Ruins

Ruins

Johnny Horn Trail

Leinster Bay

Waterlemon Beach

Leinster Bay Trail

Centerline Road

CORAL BAY

Bordeaux Mountain Trail

Mary's Creek

Annaberg Ruins

Fredricksdahl Ruins

Kings Hill Trail

Colombo Stand

DESCENT

Francis Bay Trail

Mary Point School

Maho Bay Campground

Goat Trail

Wintberg Ruins

Centerline Road

Chateau Bordeaux

Bordeaux Mountain Road
4 WD ONLY

Mary Point

Francis Bay Beach

Little Maho Beach

Maho Bay Beach

America Hill Trail

Cinnamon Bay Trail

Reef

Reef Bay Great House

Petroglyphs

Whistling Cay

Cinnamon Bay Beach

Peter Bay Beach

North Shore Rd.

Nature Trail

Ruins

Overlook

John's Head Road
4 WD ONLY

Catherineberg Ruins

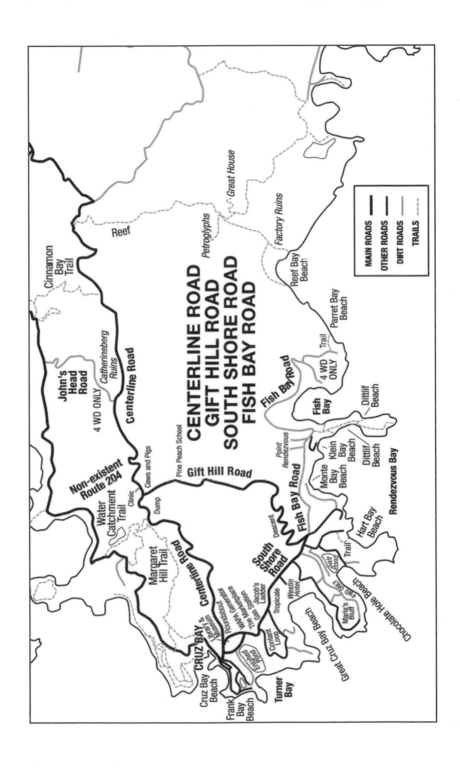

# TOUR # 2: SALT POND
## CENTERLINE ROAD / SALT POND ROAD / LAMESHUR ROAD

## CENTERLINE ROAD

### SET MILEAGE TO ZERO
The starting point for this trip is the corner of the Dolphin Market building closest to the Roundabout. Set your mileage counter to zero and continue going straight up the hill.

Centerline Road is the most direct way to get across the island, but not the most scenic. Some of the sights are covered in the North Shore trip, but I'll go over them again here.

On the left, just past Dolphin Market and St. John is the three story **Islandia Building.** Inside is the Consulate of Finland, which is the only foreign government so far that considers St. John important enough to need a consulate or embassy.

Heading out of town, is a sharp bend to the left (0.2 mi). If you were going too fast you might have ended up on the road going straight, which leads to the Cruz Bay Villas and some other houses. Just past the curve is a large, blue water tank. This is part of a new water storage system to try to help with our chronic water shortage problem. We are now connected to the St. Thomas water supply via an underwater pipe to Redhook. But that hasn't solved our water problems because the electric plant of St. Thomas is so decrepit, it frequently breaks down and cannot generate enough power to run the St. Thomas reverse osmosis plant. SO once again we have no water.

### BETHANY
Continuing along on the left at .04 miles is **Steve Black's Bridge.** This is a very impressive bridge, built by a private citizen who wanted an easier way to get home. You are supposed to sign a waiver of liability with him before using the bridge. Past that is the old road that Steve didn't like, then another flat road (.06 miles) that is a residential area with lots of kids and Prince's very nice garden project that is producing an amazing amount of food.

After the next sharp turn is **Pastory Gardens** (0.8mi). This complex has a Miniature Golf Course and a restaurant that sometimes is and sometimes isn't open. The Butterfly Museum that they were supposed to build never happened. And after getting a zoning variance by convincing the neighbors they only wanted to build a little tourist attraction, they are now trying to sell it to developers to build an 6-STOREY apartment house! The road to the right leads to the beautiful and historic **Bethany Moravian Church.**

Then comes the telephone satellite dish. This is the dish on which all our phone calls get bounced over from St. Thomas.

Every time I pass by this dish, it reminds me of Hurricane Hugo. After being hard-hit by Hurricane Hugo, St. Johnians waited patiently for someone to remember that we existed. We were very excited when the VI telephone company finally showed up. Unfortunately, they only came over to take our dish away. It seems St. Thomas only had about 2000 phones working and needed another dish. We had zero phones working and yet had to wait another few weeks to get a different dish.

In the meantime, we solved the problem in typical St. John fashion. We gave our list of family members to contact (and a short message) to either a man who used his marine radio to get the VI Marine Operator to place the call, or to another man with a cellular phone who could access the Tortola phone system by standing on the top of Bordeaux Mountain.

## PASTORY

Next comes more speed bumps, then a dirt road to the left leading to Pastory Estate Condominiums and a very, very sharp right hand turn know as Supreme Corner(1.0 mi). Trucks have to back up to make this turn, so give them room to maneuver. Just past the turn is the home turf of a large herd of goats. They have the right of way, but are pretty good about moving out off the road. After a few more turns, the horizon opens up to a panoramic view of the dump (1.3 mi).

The company that put out the dump fire had to move every inch of that hillside. They would dig up one section, spray it with foam, then move it to another section – quite an earthmoving operation on that steep incline! As you can see, the VI Government never got around to doing the last phase of the fire extinguishing operation – putting on the permanent cap (another layer of a special kind of dirt) and planting the area with trees so that one day it will blend in with the rest of the island. Instead they are once again using it as a dump.

## WATER CATCHMENT TRAIL

As the road swings wide around the dump, there is a small area to pull over on the left (1.5 mi). At the moment there is no sign to tell you this is the beginning of the Water Catchment Trail, but it is the only place along here wide enough to get off the road.

Not many people use this trail, so it might be a little bushy, but you can make it. The Water Catchment Trail is an easy hike down to the North Shore Road. Along the way it connects twice with the Margaret Hill Trail, which is a steep hike to two different summits, then down to Cruz Bay. (For details on the Water Catchment Trail see page 66, for the Margaret Hill Trail see page 73.)

## ALONG THE DUMP

All along this section of road, there are wide curves with steep dropoffs on the dump side. This makes it an ideal place for running off the road, for cars coming from Coral Bay.

St. John doesn't have very many guardrails, but we have more than we used to. In 1992, Public Works got a whole mess of rusty guardrails from somewhere. We were sure they were rejects because they were so rusty and ugly. But Public Works insisted that was what they were supposed to look like. A guardrail installation truck was borrowed from St. Croix. They set to work. Some of Gift Hill Road got done and even some of the road out on Salt Pond Road. But then the guardrail truck ran off the road right at this bend (1.6 mi), and that was the end of that project. (The driver was not hurt too bad. The truck stayed there for quite a while, but finally was hauled out and then vanished.) After a few years, Ira Wade, our very resourceful head of Public Works on St. John, painted most of the ugly guardrails with extra yellow paint – the kind used to paint the middle line in the road. The next attempt at installing guardrails went better, except in many places the shear drop is much higher than the guard rail posts. So they just skipped over these areas. Beware, a lack of guardrails does not mean no dropoff.

At the next curve is an interesting dirt road that goes almost straight up (1.8 mi). This is supposed to be the shortcut for ambulance drivers on the way to the emergency room at the clinic, but I can't imagine how they are going to keep the stretcher and patient from falling out the back door of the ambulance – look at how steep that road is!

### GIFT HILL ROAD INTERSECTION

Around the next curve is the junction of Gift Hill Road (1.8/1.9 mi). Be prepared to stop. This extremely wide intersection is a courtesy of the dump fire. It was widened for all the dump trucks. Unfortunately, no one in Public Works figured out how to use this big area effectively after its expansion, so they just painted the lines where they were originally supposed to go when the road was skinny. Tony decided to solve the problem by setting up his BBQ van. Now he and his customers use up quite a lot of the extra space, especially on weekend nights when there is a full house for the (illegal) cockfights. It can be a little chaotic around here – go slow and pay attention.

Now you are on the section of road covered in detail in the North Shore trip, so I will just briefly cover them here.

### CLINIC, PIGS AND COWS

On your left is the **Myrah Keating Smith Community Health Center** (2.0 mi). Just past the clinic and Paradise Lumber on the left is the dirt road that leads to the non-existent Route 204 – this is a totally impassable donkey trail in spite of what the VI government map says. Next is a Laundromat, Car Wash (2.2 mi) and various construction projects of a gentleman named Iva Moses.

This area has a high-density population of cows and pigs. One of the pigs has learned how to get milk from a cooperative cow. Next to Moses' property is the Majestic Company, currently closed.

## CATHERINEBERG, JOHN'S HEAD ROAD

This section is know as the "straight away"– the only place on St. John where you can shift into fourth gear – for all of 3 seconds. At the curve that ends this almost straight section of road, is a dirt road to the left, with a large sign saying VI National Park. This is a nice sign but it doesn't help you know that this is the Catherineberg – John's Head Road (3.0 mi), the mostly unpaved 4WD track that leads down to the North Shore Road and also to the beautiful windmill at the Hammer Farm ruins, just a short way down the road.

## CENTERLINE OVERLOOK, CINNAMON BAY TRAIL

Next is an overlook on the left (3.6 mi) with a great view of the North Shore and a sign identifying all the islands you can see.

As you go down the hill, there will be a large number 4 painted on the road. This is a mile marker for our annual **8 Tuff Miles Race.** These mile markers are completely different from both the signposted numbers and my mileage numbers. But they make good reference points. On the opposite side of the road from the number 4, look around to find the trail that goes in to some excellent ruins – this is **Estate Rustenburg.**

At the bottom of this hill is the Cinnamon Bay Trailhead (3.9 mi) that has room for a few cars across from the trail (for details see page 70).

## REEF BAY TRAIL

Centerline Road continues climbing and winding with glimpses of the North Shore to your left and the South Shore to your right. Except in one spot where the road actually twists all the way around until the water you see on your right is the North Shore! Can you find this spot? It is much easier to find this when you are walking. Look really hard a few curves before you get to the very sharp switchback; the best viewing spot is right by a large dent in the guardrail.

After the really sharp switchback, the road descends. At the very bottom of the hill is the beginning of the Reef Bay Trail (4.8 mi). Start this very popular trail by going down the stairs in the stone wall on the right. You can park your car somewhere on the left or just past the trail on the right. (For details see page 75.)

## CHATEAU BORDEAUX

After a few more switchbacks, you come to the highest point of Centerline Road and a magnificent view of Coral Bay, Hurricane Hole, the East End, and the British Virgin Islands (5.0 mi). The Chateau Bordeaux Restaurant is the very best place to take in the view – stop for lunch or a drink (say Hi to Lorelei for me). The paved road going up the hill off to the right is the Bordeaux Mountain Road (only the first ¼ mile is paved).

Along the next stretch of road on the left are cotton bushes left over from the plantation days (5.2-5.4 mi). These tall bushes are covered with little white cotton balls when in bloom.

## NORTH SHORE ROAD INTERSECTION

At the Colombo Yogurt stand and the intersection of the North Shore Road (5.9 mi), go straight. It's all downhill to Coral Bay from here. Don't get going too fast, there are some sharp curves along the way, and watch out for herds of goats.

This is the beginning of two sections of Centerline Road have been renamed Gerda Marsh Drive and the Marsh's Scenic Highway. This was part of the agreement made in the 1970's when the Marsh family sold their land to the government to allow Centerline Road to extend all the way to Coral Bay.

Frequently, there is a bulldozer sitting on the side of the road just past the where the 8 Tuff Mile Race marker number 6 painted on the road. Lately, some creative person has taken to decorating it for holidays – a wreath for Christmas, hearts for Valentine's Day, etc. It may be the same person that saw a cement truck broken down near Concordia and painted it into a beautiful, enormous, Easter Egg (it has since been moved to Rupert's junk yard and can be admired there – go past the Love City Mini Mart, past the goat pen and look on the left for the Easter Egg).

Take the time to appreciate the absolutely spectacular views of Coral Bay by pulling over into the turnouts. One of the best view spots is from the large boulders at **Yucca Point** (6.7mi). Yuccas are those tall plants with the long, bayonet shaped green leaves. The white flower petals are edible.

## CORAL BAY TRIANGLE

Once the road levels off at sea level, you come to the "Triangle" intersection in Coral Bay (7.8 mi). To the right is the road to Salt Pond (route 107), straight ahead goes to the East End (more of route 10).

## SALT POND ROAD

Set your trip meter to zero, all mileage readings start from here. Turn right onto the Salt Pond Road – route 107. Actually this road does not seem to have a name, but since it does go to the Salt Pond and everyone knew which road I was talking about when I tested it out, this name will do.

There is a wide space along the side of the playing field fence where it looks like the road thought about going that way once, then changed its mind. This is now the overflow parking area for major events in Coral Bay and is sometimes the location for flea markets and garage sales. There are a few mobile food carts located here that have very tasty food if you can figure out when they are going to be open. A little further down the road on the right is a wooden building currently housing a gift shop, but still referred to as Pickles Deli which closed down years ago.

## DOMINO GAS STATION

On the right is the Domino Gas Station – currently closed. We are all very happy to get a gas station in Coral Bay but were very surprised that anyone could get a permit to build underground gas tanks in a mangrove swamp – one leak and there goes this delicate eco-system.

## LOVE CITY MINI MART ROAD INTERSECTION

The first road on the right (0.2 mi) leads to the **Savers Market,** a very nice little general store. Beware of inaccurate route signs: this road does not lead to any usable road back to Cruz Bay. It does lead to the turnoff for the almost-always impassable dirt road coming down from Bordeaux Mountain, and it also goes straight past **Josephine's farm** (excellent place to by greens and some veggies) to the bottom of the always impassable Kings Hill Trail.

Each community in the Virgin Islands has an outdoor meeting place for hanging out and talking, and Coral Bay's spot is under the trees at the entrance to this road. There are plans to make the whole corner lot into a botanical garden. The large wooden spool is the dominoes table. Across the street are large dumpsters. St. John does not have a home pickup garbage service; everyone hauls their garbage to a dumpster like this. Then a truck comes around, loads it all up and takes it to the dump.

This system is much appreciated by the mongooses, dogs, and cats that use it as a primary food source, also by new residents who are happy to recycle anything – this dumpster and the one in Chocolate Hole have the reputation of being excellent for scavenging.

This area is home to a large herd of goats and another herd of sheep. St. John sheep are not the classic wooly variety – in fact the sheep look almost exactly like the goats. The only way to tell the different is: if the tail goes up it is a goat, if the tail hangs down it is a sheep.

## CLAM DIP

Then comes the "Clam Dip" (0.3 mi) - this can literally rip the bottom off your car, so slow down. Since you are already going slow, take a good look at the **mangrove swamp.** The mangroves are trees that are capable of growing in brackish and salty water because they sweat out the salt through their leaves and bark. Roots are sent out in all directions creating a filter and trap for sediment being washed down the hillsides. Eventually, enough soil and debris will accumulate to create solid land and new water front acreage, with the mangroves moving further and further out into the bay. The swamp is home to a huge variety of baby sea life and is also well-loved by mosquitoes. The large holes are homes for **land crabs** that can get up to 9 inches across and are equipped with a large, effective claws. These crabs make very good eating once you clean them out for a week or so by feeding them corn meal.

## A CLUSTER OF BUSINESSES

Around the bend is a paved road going off to the right. This is Lower Bordeaux Mountain Road (also called "Costanzo's" Road). It is finally completely paved all the way up to the mountaintop , but it still can require four-wheel drive when wet.

To the left, a little further on (0.5mi) is a restaurant that has been changing owners frequently. At the moment it is a bar/restaurant called **Island Blues.** Then comes a very large closed restaurant on the right – formerly Voyages, then a small mall-type area with **Aqua Bistro** restaurant, **Lily's Market,** retail shops and a water-toy rental place called **Crabby's.** (See Update chapter for more information about this area).

After all this congestion (according to Coral Bay standards) the road climbs and winds along the coast. It is easy to follow if you go slowly.

There is one curve (1.0 mi) where the road goes sharply to the left and a very steep new cement driveway is straight ahead. It's possible to mistakenly end up on the driveway instead of the road. This can happen at a few more places along this road. If you end up on the driveways, you can either pretend you really wanted to go that way or just look sheepish, back up and try again.

## SHIPWRECK RESTAURANT

The next cluster of houses is Freeman's Ground on Johnson Bay. Here you can find Shipwreck Restaurant and some interesting gift shops (1.6 mi) here. This area got its name because when the plantations were shutting down, this very poor land was given to the freed slaves. Actually, this whole coastline has wonderful names that describe the infertile land, like John's Folly and Hard Labor.

## JOHNSON BAY

Across the street from the restaurant, that bay and the one around the corner to the right are both considered Johnson Bay. The very rocky beach is not the prettiest swimming or snorkeling spot, but there is a reef way over to the right of the far-right cove that you could try. A short walk up and over the hill is a section of beach with a bit of sand that might be more appealing. (For details see page 47.)

A little further, past yet another enormous construction site is a paved road to the left leading to the Johnson Bay subdivision (2.0 mi). They do not want you to use their road to access Johnson Bay Beach. Instead, walk down the dirt road just before it to get to the bay.

## MISS LUCY'S, FRIIS BAY BEACH

After a few more hills and turns you come to another little community at Friis Bay (2.6 mi). The only tourist attraction here is **Miss Lucy's Restaurant** (2.8 mi), a traditional West Indian restaurant right on the sea. The beach in front of Miss Lucy's is sand and there are some reefs out there to the left, but it is not known as a great snorkeling location. The full moon parties are well worth attending. (For details see page 47.)

## JOHN'S FOLLY

Just past Miss Lucy's is another tricky curve. The road going straight is the driveway of the **Calvary Baptist Church.** You want to go left to follow the road around to John's Folly Bay (3.2 mi), which has a large herd of goats sometimes playing in the road. Don't pay any attention to the sign for Sweets Beach Bar – it was only open for about a month, 7 years ago. John's Folly is all private land and they don't encourage tourists to visit.

## CONCORDIA

At the well-marked turnoff to Concordia (3.5mi) is a new restaurant called **The Tourist Trap.** We all thought this was a very funny name but apparently tourists do not agree. Please stop in and tell Larry how you feel about the name – it is a great place to hang out, drink, eat, and gossip.

A sister to Maho Campground, Concordia offers "eco-tents" and villas. There is a swimming pool and now has a restaurant and store. Once Maho Campground's lease runs out, that entire operation will be moving over here and the facilities will increase. For now, try exploring the hiking trails down to the rocky beach, out to Nanny Point, and over to Drunk Bay and Salt Pond.

## SALT POND BAY

The road swings inland around the bay, up a long hill and then takes you back onto National Park land. The parking area for Salt Pond Bay is on the left (4.2 mi). This is the end of the bus line. Unfortunately, there have been numerous problems with thefts from cars parked here, so take everything with you. (Better yet, leave your valuables back at the hotel. Never leave your wallet or camera unattended – especially on the beach while swimming.) Sometimes there is a mobile concession stand operating here, but do not count on it – bring your own food and drink. If you are lucky, **Ital** may be selling his wood carvings and other locally made stuff next to the bus stop. The dirt road to the left leads to ruins of a small house (that I would love to live in) then continues on to Concordia.

## SALT POND BAY BEACH

The trail leading to Salt Pond Beach is the one with the bar across it. It is about a 5-minute walk down the hill to the wide, sandy beach. There are a few picnic tables, an outhouse, and not too much shade. This gorgeous bay is excellent for snorkeling and is the starting point for the Drunk Bay Beach Trail and the Ram Head Trail. (For beach details see page 47.)

## DRUNK BAY TRAIL AND BEACH

The Drunk Bay Trail is a short, easy trail along the salt pond that crosses over to the ocean. The coastline here is wild and rugged. It is not good for swimming, but it's great for beachcombing and sculpture-building. (For details see pages 47 and 67.)

## RAM HEAD TRAIL

The Ram Head trail is an excellent hike through the dry forest and out to the

Ram Head point. There is a rocky beach, Ram Head Trail Beach, along the way, to swim or snorkel. The trail involves some climbing and it's hot – bring lots of water. The view from the top, of the waves bashing against the cliffs, is well worth the sweat. (For trail details see page 70, for beach details see page 48.)

# LAMESHUR ROAD

### END OF PAVEMENT
Continue on the road until the pavement ends (4.6 mi). From here on to Lameshur Bay you *should* have four-wheel drive. The terrible hill has finally been paved, but other parts of the road are not and you may need four-wheel drive to make it safely especially after it rains when large portions of the road are under water. Take note that some of the car rental companies ask you not to take their cars down this road. Just before the beginning of the hill (5.3 mi), there is a good place to leave your car on the side of the road and walk.

### GREAT LAMESHUR BEACH
After ascending and descending the steep hill, continue along the flats to a small opening on the left under an enormous Tamarind tree (5.2 mi). This is Great Lameshur Bay beach – a rocky beach good for swimming, snorkeling, and beachcombing. There is no way to walk along this beach and over to the dock (for details see page 48). But you can walk/scramble along the coast to the left for a long ways.

### VIERS
Further down, the road follows along a large mangrove swamp. The dirt road to the right (5.5 mi) leads to VIERS **(Virgin Islands Ecological Research Station)**, and they don't mind visitors. This collection of buildings was built by the U.S. Navy while they were conducting some early underwater living experiments. In a corner of Great Lameshur Bay, they sunk an underwater pod called Tektite, and people lived within it for months. It is too bad they hauled it away. The camp is now used by different research and educational groups. There are dormitory-type buildings, a kitchen and dining building, electricity and even (gasp!) a public pay telephone.

When the fruit is ripe, the large mango tree is boldly patronized by the normally shy deer and wild pigs. Actually, there are a few lazy deer who have learned that hanging out near the kitchen and mooching from visitors is an easy way to get fed – they have become almost permanent residents of VIERS.

### YAWZI POINT TRAIL
The next turnoff to the left (5.7 mi) leads to the Yawzi trailhead. The small building on the edge of Great Lameshur Bay is the VIERS lab. There is also a dock. Where the road turns to the left is the beginning of the Yawzi Trail. It is a short easy trail that goes out to the point and the ruins of the **Quarantine camp.**

There is a great snorkel spot along the way. (For details see page 63.)

## LITTLE LAMESHUR BEACH

The beach at Lameshur (actually it's Little Lameshur Bay, but so few people go to Great Lameshur that this is known as Lameshur) is easy to spot. It comes right up to the road (5.7 mi). This beautiful sandy beach has good swimming and snorkeling, and it is usually not very crowded. (For details see page 49.)

## LAMESHUR RUINS

Past the beach is the end of the road (5.8 mi). To the left, jutting out into the bay is the ruins of a small house. Don't fall into the exposed cistern. Those boiling vats were used to extract the oil from **Bay Rum leaves.** Someday, the National Park is going to restore these ruins, which would be nice.

The grassy area on the inland side of these buildings is a very good place to go spider fishing. Look for holes in the ground about 1½ inch wide – the bigger the hole the better. Find a long blade of grass and stick the grass down the hole. Wiggle it some until you feel something grab the grass. Now very slowly try to bring the brown hairy ground spider to the surface. You only get one or maybe two tries before the spider gets sick of this game and won't play anymore – pick another hole and try again. (Warning: don't try to pick up these spiders with bare hands – they might bite).

## BORDEAUX MOUNTAIN TRAIL

The path to the right is the Bordeaux Mountain Trail. It is wide enough for a car to go up as far as the ranger's house, then it turns into a foot trail. Starting from here is the hard way to hike this trail. It goes straight up to 1277 feet in 1.2 hot steep miles. (For details see page 71.)

## LAMESHUR BAY TRAIL

Straight ahead, with the chain across it, is the Lameshur Bay Trail. It goes over the hills to connect with the Reef Bay Trail (1.8 mi) and to a small spur trail going to Europa Bay. If you haven't been to Reef Bay yet, here's your chance. (For details see page 71.)

## EUROPA BAY TRAIL AND BEACH

The Europa Bay Trail turns off from the Lameshur Trail after about 0.3 miles. It leads to a large salt pond that is very good for bird and duck watching, especially early in the morning and late in the afternoon. Then it continues on to Europa Bay Beach, which is only good for swimming and snorkeling on very calm days, but is very good for beachcombing all the time. (For trail details see page 67, for beach details page 49).

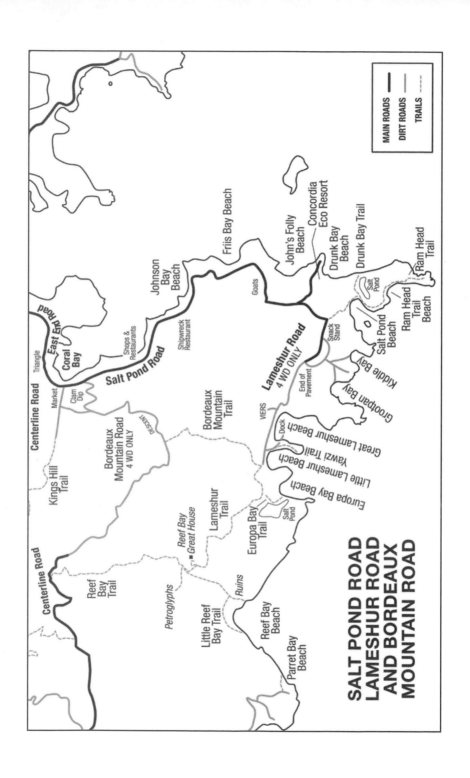

SALT POND ROAD
LAMESHUR ROAD
AND BORDEAUX
MOUNTAIN ROAD

MAIN ROADS
DIRT ROADS
TRAILS

Centerline Road

Kings Hill
Trail

Reef
Bay
Trail

Centerline Road

Market

Triangle

East End Road

Coral
Bay

Clam
Dip

Shops &
Restaurants

Johnson
Bay
Beach

Shipwreck
Restaurant

Salt Pond Road

Bordeaux
Mountain Road
4 WD ONLY

DESCENT

Friis Bay Beach

Goats

Bordeaux
Mountain
Trail

Lameshur Road
4 WD ONLY

VIERS

End of
Pavement

John's Folly
Beach

Concordia
Eco Resort

Drunk Bay
Beach

Drunk Bay Trail

Ram Head
Trail

Salt
Pond

Ram Head
Trail Beach

Salt Pond
Beach

Snack
Stand

Kiddle Bay

Grootpan Bay

Dock

Great Lameshur Beach

Yawzi Trail

Little Lameshur Beach

Europa Bay Beach

Lameshur
Trail

Reef Bay
Great House

Europa Bay
Trail

Salt
Pond

Petroglyphs

Ruins

Little Reef
Bay Trail

Reef Bay
Beach

Parret Bay
Beach

# TOUR #3: EAST END
# CORAL BAY AND EAST END ROAD

Mileage readings start from the Triangle in Coral Bay.

## CORAL BAY

Coral Bay is a very small community on the "other side" of St. John. The people here consider Cruz Bay the big city. They've been known to talk of Coral Bay seceding and declaring itself its own country or maybe putting up a big gate on Centerline Road to only allow Coral Bay'ers in. The community has a fire station, a school, a few small food stores, bars, restaurants, a gas station, and a few shops.

Coral Bay was the original settlement on St. John and, during the plantation days, over half the population of St. John lived here. The low flatlands had pens for cattle called *corrals,* which was eventually corrupted into Coral and became the name we use today. After the U.S. bought the islands, the population center shifted to the closest point between St. Thomas and St. John – Cruz Bay.

The entire bay is named Coral Bay, with different sections being **Hurricane Hole, Round Bay, and Coral Harbor.** The bay is wide and deep, with lots of hidden inlets. This makes it an excellent hiding place for boats during hurricanes. Hundreds of boats come here for each storm and most of them survive. Some of those that didn't can still be seen littering the shoreline.

## MORAVIAN CHURCH

Going straight at the Triangle, the Moravian Church is on the hill to the left. This beautiful building, built in 1726, is one of the oldest structures on the island. It was destroyed in the 1916 hurricane, but has since been rebuilt. It is still in use today. Everyone is welcome to join in the Sunday morning services. While many of the other religions that came to St. John were aimed at saving the souls of the plantation owners, the Moravians came to bring Christianity to the slaves. They often held services in the fields and were the only faith willing to baptize children born out of wedlock.

## JOHNNY HORN TRAIL

The driveway of the Moravian Church is the trailhead for the Johnny Horn Trail – that's the unmaintained one that may or may not require a whole team of machete-wielding hikers to negotiate easily. It leads over to Waterlemon Beach and Annaberg. (For details see page 73.)

## SPUTNIKS

Across from the church is the **Guy Benjamin School** and the playing field (lots of school kids is the reason for the three speed bumps, please go slow). The **Sputniks** complex is on the left: Sputniks is the bar, next door is the **Donkey Diner.** More name games – this use to be the P&B Diner, which became the

M&M Donkey Diner but is now simply the Donkey Diner because the two M's sold it to non-M people. Anyway, it is the only place in Coral Bay serving breakfast, and also offers pizza a few nights a week and a great BBQ on Saturday night.

Sputniks is a great place to find people who might be willing to tell stories about the good old days, before Coral Bay got so crowded. For dancers and music lovers, Sputniks is the Coral Bay equivalent of **Fred's,** but not quite so predictable: ask about the current entertainment schedule.

## SKINNY LEGS

Next comes the fire station (which has given up on making its ATM machine work at the moment), then a new building on the left that was supposed to be a grocery store but that never happened. Instead **Marla** runs her custom embroidery shop on the ground floor – she is very friendly, stop in and say hi.

On the right side of the road is the **Wall Street Complex** with some terrific shops, **Connections East** (newspapers, communications services, day sail reservations, Internet access, plus tourist information), a leather shop and **Skinny Legs Bar.** Skinny's bills itself as a "pretty OK place with same-day service." It has excellent hamburgers. The TV's are always tuned to the sports channel, and the bar is usually filled with friendly folks. It is easy to hustle up a game of darts or horseshoes here and there is plenty of room for the kids to run around. During season you can come dance to live music on Saturday nights. Throughout the year, Monday is movie night. If you happen to see the sole remaining owner, you can look down and see how accurately the bar is named.

The extraordinary "recycled junk" sculptures decorating the bar are the work of **Kevin** the cook who has unfortunately moved off-island. He also created the sign out front where you can stick your head in the hole to get your picture taken with skinny legs, put the Skinny Legs bench –complete with socks– up at the Triangle, and created the turtle on the road side past Haulover. We miss his creativity.

Behind Skinny's is **Coral Bay Marine.** A very impressive name for a small dinghy dock, a flat place to haul your boat, (no, the lift doesn't work) and a marine supply store. There is a large live-aboard boating community out there in the bay.

## FORTSBERG HILL

Past Skinny's the road goes by a salt flat (usually dried out), then comes to a large stone building on the right – the **Flamingo Club** (0.4 mi), a night club that is only opened for special occasions. The bus turns around here, heads back to the triangle then continues out to Salt Pond.

Follow the dirt road to find **Donkey Dana** of Coral Bay Corral for a wonderful horse or donkey trail rides.

The hill behind the bar is Fortsberg Hill, location of the fort that was overtaken by the slaves as the first act in the revolt of 1733. Even though the park maps show the hill as being within their boundaries, it is private land and sightseers are not welcome without permission from the owners.

## ESTATE ZOOTENVAAL

The road climbs up a hill, then abruptly goes steeply down again and around a very sharp corner (go slow and use low gear) into the Borck Creek section of Hurricane Hole. The cluster of small tourist cottages is Estate Zootenvaal (0.9 mi). Zootenvaal has a small sandy beach that is fenced off. It is difficult to access the water along this bay, but if you really wanted to, you could pick your way through the mangroves to the water. The next bay offers easier access to mangrove snorkeling. All along this bay and the next you will see lots of clothes in the bushes, discarded by the illegal aliens who have been dropped off from a boat.

## HERMITAGE RUINS, BROWN BAY TRAIL

Next, the road crosses one of the very few bridges on St. John, and definitely one of the most impressive (1.2 mi). It is actually recognizable as a bridge. Just past the bridge is a dirt road to the left that leads to the Hermitage ruins and the beginning of the Brown Bay Trail. This is another unmaintained trail that may or may not be overgrown. It goes over to Brown Bay and then to Annaberg. (For details see page 74.)

## PRINCESS BAY

Once again, you go up and over a steep hill to Princess Bay and the St. John Quarter Mile Speed Way (1.8 mi). This is the longest, straightest stretch of road on the island and drag racing can be happening at any time. Be extra careful.

Princess Bay doesn't really have a beach, but it does have access to some unique mangrove snorkeling. Don't knock it until you've tried it. Mangrove snorkeling may sound horrible, but it can be absolutely fascinating. (For more details, see page 50.)

## HAULOVER BAY

At the top of the next hill (2.5 mi) there are a series of dirt lookout areas on the left with great views of Tortola. This is also the end of the National Park. Down at the bottom is Haulover Bay (3.2 mi). The large tree on the road with Vie's sign on it is a **Tamarind tree.** Break open the brown pods to find the gooey seeds that are a bit tart, but make a delicious drink if you boil them like tea. This is the "secret" ingredient in Worcestershire Sauce.

Haulover is the very lowest, narrowest land on the East End. The local fishermen used to haul their long boats over this land to go to Tortola, rather than row all the way around East End, thus the name Haulover Bay.

Haulover Beach South is on the right. This beach is popular because it is the closest beach to Coral Bay. It offers good swimming and snorkeling.

On the left of the road is a trail (no sign, but it's easy to find) leading to Haulover Beach North on the Drake's Passage side. This rocky beach frequently has choppy waves, which usually prohibits any attempt to go snorkel the excellent reefs. There is also a small sandy beach further down that involves some rock scrambling to reach. (For beach details see page 50.)

## VIE'S

Back on the road, just past Haulover on the left, look for the large rock, cleverly transformed by an artist to be a turtle. A local resident likes to decorate this turtle with seasonally appropriate hats and flags – St. Paddies Day is a big event.

After conquering the next hill you come to Limetree Cove (3.8 mi) with the two large trees in the middle of the road and **Vie's Snack Stand** (open irregularly but definitely worth a stop if it is – superb pates). The beach has been fenced off. Miss Vie's has turned her section of the beachfront into a campground (very basic) and charges you a fee to use the beach.

## HANSEN BAY BEACH

Over the next hill is Hansen Bay (4.0 mi) where there is access to the beach. This is another small, mostly rocky beach with good swimming and excellent snorkeling out to Pelican Rock. (For details see page 51.)

## LONG BAY BEACH

Up and over the next hill go past the dirt road going to the left (the sign says Privateer Estate), keep going straight down to the end of the pavement to find access to another beach (4.2 mi). Park out of the way of the private driveways and follow the little path to the mostly-rocky Long Bay Beach, which is another starting point to snorkel out to Pelican Rock. (For details see page 51.)

## PRIVATEER BAY BEACH

Going back the way you came, the dirt road turnoff on the right first passes the **Sloop Jones workshop** – a great place to stop to see a St. John artist at work creating gorgeous handpainted clothing. The road continues to 2 different roads: the one to the right goes less than a mile further out on the East End, then dead ends. This road offers some breathtaking views and a lot of bumps and potholes, but no more beaches.

The other road goes through the Privateer Estate subdivision. This paved road was the cause of controversy – apparently there is a species of bush that does not exist anywhere in the world except out here in this very dry isolated area.

Unfortunately, by the time this was announced, "Dozer Tom" had already been let loose and had finished the road. There is still plenty of room for the bush to grow as long as the new homebuilders don't clear it all away.

The view at the top of the hill is spectacular and, if you have four-wheel drive, it's possible to continue on and drive *steeply* down to the Privateer Bay Beach – a rocky beach with good snorkeling. This very, very steep hill, however, is difficult to get back up after even a slight rain.

Note that if you get stuck, this is a long way from everywhere and the odds of anyone passing by to help are very slim. (For beach details see page 51.)

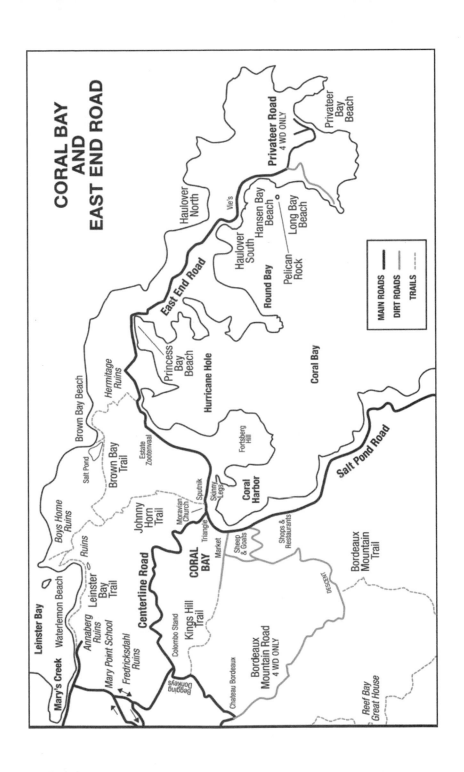

# TOUR #4: FISH BAY ROAD

Mileage readings start from the turnoff onto the dirt Fish Bay Road from the intersection of the South Shore and Gift Hill Roads.

Fish Bay Road is now paved. It is technically a private road. The VI Government map doesn't even show it exists. The Fish Bay Owners Association has done a great job of paving a few more feet of it whenever they can afford to – while continuing in their attempts to get the VI Government to claim responsibility for it.

## POINT RENDEZVOUS

The first section of the road was cut into the hillside and follows the contours of Rendezvous Bay at about 200 feet above sea level. Various private driveways shoot off from it to the right. The turnoff to the left (0.5 mi) is the very impressive entrance (one of three) to Point Rendezvous – a new subdivision.

## KLEIN BAY BEACH

The next turn to the right (.06 mi) is a paved road leading to a batch of new vacation rental houses, then down to the stony Klein Bay Beach. Snorkeling here is good but not spectacular, the swimming is fine. Occasionally there are dolphins and whales in this bay. (For details see page 55.)

## DITTLIF POINT TRAIL AND BEACHES

Back on the main road, there used to be room to park a few cars at the next curve halfway down the steep hill (0.7 mi). But the developers installed massive boulders to keep people from doing that. Sometimes you can drive down the road to the Dittlif Point trails to the beaches, or you can park at the very bottom of the hill. This is a hot, dry hike that goes to some beaches on the Fish Bay side which offer great snorkeling for those who are not intimidated by sharks. There is also a beach on the Rendezvous Bay side that does not have sharks. (For trail details see page 68, for beaches page 55.)

## FISH BAY

Once back on the road, it drops down to sea level and you are in Fish Bay. This bay is a mangrove swamp and very shallow. It is good for fishing and mosquitoes and sharks, but not so good for swimming. Continue along the main road, Marina Road. Follow the edge of the mangrove swamp while ignoring the side roads leading up to private homes. (Fish Bay is one of the few places on St. John with street signs. Isn't it nice?).

At the Fish Bay Gut, there is a bridge (1.1 mi) with wooden railings. If you have a desire to experience walking through a mangrove swamp, walk down the gut to the right for a little ways. Walking the other way up the Gut is an EXTREMELY difficult Off-the-Trail hike.

## PARRET BAY

Further on, Marina Road goes to the right and Reef Bay Road goes straight (1.8 mi). Go straight, up the paved section, then be ready for a turn to the left (1.9 mi). Hilltop Road goes straight, Reef Bay goes left. The road gets pretty rough; you might need 4WD. Continue on until the road widens a little near a telephone pole next to a house with shingles (2.1 mi). This is the parking area for the trail down to the Parret Bay beach.

This is not an easy trail – note the knotted rope that you use to descend/ascend – but it does get you down to that nice-looking sandy beach.

There are reefs protecting the beach, but since it faces straight out to sea, usually there are waves pounding the coral. Snorkeling here can be dangerous. When the waves are really big, all the surfers come here. It is possible to scramble around the rocky point to the Little Reef Bay Trail and get over to the main Reef Bay Trail beach (For beach details see page 55, trail details see page 72). That's it for the sights of Fish Bay.

# TOUR #5: BORDEAUX MOUNTAIN ROAD

A portion of the Bordeaux Mountain Road has been paved, but not all of it, and the last part of it is extremely dangerous. This means you have to drive your jeep back out the same way you went in. Only hikers should do the entire road.

The unpaved part is in pretty good shape out to the Bordeaux Mountain Trailhead except for one patch of clay that is very slippery whenever it rains. A little way past the trail and a house, you will come to the treacherous descent to Coral Bay which has finally been paved, but still requires four-wheel drive whenever the pavement is even slightly damp.

I highly recommend doing the entire road as a hike, since the fairly flat road travels through a beautiful shady tropical forest to the summit, then descends through dry scrub with great views all the way down to Coral Bay. The walking time is about 1 ½ hours. Plan to meet your car in a Coral Bay bar or ride the bus back up Centerline Road.

## CHATEAU BORDEAUX

From the Chateau Bordeaux group of shops, follow the pavement up the hill and along the mountain ridge through a beautiful forest of tall trees. After you pass the sign for a subdivision on your left there is nothing but trees and birds for about a mile. The **St. John Audubon Society** has placed birdhouses in the trees, but they are extremely difficult to spot. At the Y-intersection that usually has a dead end sign on it (1.1 mi), the pavement goes down a hill – don't go that way, bear to the right and soon the pavement runs out.

## BORDEAUX MOUNTAIN TRAIL

Continue on the dirt road, hopefully getting past the slippery clay part successfully, and you'll come to the Bordeaux Mountain Trail Head just past the telephone pole labeled ES50 on the right-hand side (1.7 mi). This trail leads down to Lameshur Bay, dropping 1200 feet in 1.2 miles. It would be nice if you had a car waiting down there for you so you don't have to climb back up. (For details see page 71). On the opposite side of the road from the beginning of the trail are some ruins that you might want to poke around.

## BORDEAUX MOUNTAIN LOOKOUT

The road continues up to the summit of Bordeaux Mountain, the highest point on St. John, and then starts to descend. There is a good lookout point before it starts to get really steep (2.1 mi). Get out and have a look at the view then turn around and go back the way you came if you don't have 4-wheel drive.

## THE DESCENT

The road goes down steeply with lots of switchbacks. If you follow the paved part all the way down the hill you will end up connecting with Salt Pond Road near Island Blues restaurant. If you take a dirt road to the left, there will a lot of switchbacks before you eventually come to the valley floor and a T-intersection at Rupert's Junkyard. Turn right and after about 1 mile you will go past Love City Mini Mart and connect with Salt Pond Road right in the middle of the mangrove swamp.

# TOUR #6: CRUZ BAY "BACKSIDE"

## ENIGHED POND/TURNER BAY/FRANK BAY

This trip could be hiked but the one horrible steep hill makes it a hard walk.

### ENIGHED POND AND TURNER BAY BEACH

In Cruz Bay, one road at the Roundabout is a turnoff to the tennis court parking lot that goes past the fire station. This is part of the South Shore Road. The main road goes left at the tennis court corner; you want to go straight onto the badly-maintained dirt road. Follow Fish Fry Drive along Enighed Pond, to Pond Mouth and the sea. This is Turner Bay. It is not good for swimming since there are large barges constantly going in and out of the cargo port

The road then turns inland, and comes to a T-intersection. Carefully, without bumping into the iron post, go left. Continue on around to another pond that is called Small Pond.

This pond is a declared bird sanctuary and wildlife refuge. The windsurfer floating out in the middle is not an accident, it's there for the ducks to hang out on and they love it. That windsurfer has miraculously survived all of our hurricanes! The Audubon Society has plans to replace it with a larger platform.

### THE HILL

Past the pond the road turns sharply right and wow, what a hill. I have measured the degree of incline – it's 37 degrees. U.S. highway engineers consider anything past 7 degrees to be too steep. Amazingly enough, this hill is one of the few sections of the island which is zoned for high density, and unfortunately it has been highly-developed. I have no idea how all of those buildings will get water since the water trucks cannot make it up the hill. If there is even a small amount of rain on this road you will probably not be able to get up it even with 4WD, and sliding back down is really dangerous. So only go on dry days.

Halfway up the hill on the right is the remains of one of our island disasters – a 6-unit apartment house caught fire and burned the three-unit house on one side and the three-unit house on the other. The fire trucks couldn't get re-supplied with water because the hill was wet and the trucks were too big to get around the corner past that iron post coming the other way.

### GENIP STREET

Before you get to the top of the hill, beep your horn to let people know you're coming. If you go straight, you'll end up right back in Cruz Bay next to the school. Or you can go left onto Genip Street. Genip winds past some vacation condo rental complexes (Battery Hill, Conch Villas, Lavender Hill) before coming to Gallows Point, then past the cemetery and back into Cruz Bay by Wharfside Village.

## FRANK BAY BEACH

The road to the left off of Genip, just as you get to the sea, takes you down to Frank Bay Beach. The cute little house right across the road from the beach is the **Coconut Coast Art Gallery**. This gallery is open to the public and invites everyone to nice cocktail parties with live music every Wednesday evening in season (say Hi to Elaine for me).

The beach is mostly rocks with little patches of sand, and the reef is almost on shore which makes it very hard to get into the water. Watch out, there are lots of urchins. Otherwise, the snorkeling is very good. At the end of the beach and up the hill past the now-unused reverse osmosis plant, is **Patrick's food stand** (ask when he is going to have a fish fry). Access to it and out on Moorehead Point used to be seriously prohibited, but now that Mrs. Moorehead died, it is OK to go up to eat at Patrick's. (For beach details see page 53.)

## GALLOWS POINT

Just before the cemetery is Gallows Point. This is a condo hotel: each unit is owned by different people who then let the association rent it out like a hotel room. The complex has **Zozo's Restaurant** (the bar on the top floor offers great sunset and green flash viewing), a swimming pool, a small rocky beach and a gift shop. The management says they don't want non-guests walking through their grounds, but, again, all beaches must be accessible to the public by law.

# TOUR #7: EXTRAS

If you've been on all the other roads and you still want to snoop around some more, here are two more loops, nothing very exciting, but they do exist.

## CHOCOLATE HOLE/MARIA BLUFF

Coming from Cruz Bay on the South Shore Road, just up the hill from the Westin, is a paved road to the right. This is Great Cruz Bay Road. Follow this road all the way along the point over a million speed bumps, and eventually it loops around to the Chocolate Hole side and turns into dirt – not very well-maintained and usually washed-out. The road comes back along the bay to connect up again with the South Shore Road. The dirt road portion requires decent four-wheel drive expertise.

## CONTANT

Coming from Cruz Bay along the South Shore Road, before the E&C gas station is a road to the right next to the basketball courts. This road goes past the basketball courts, then up a long hill, around Contant Point, back along the Great Cruz Bay side and reconnects with the South Shore Road at the top of Jacob's Ladder. When accidents close Jacob's ladder (a frequent occurrence and usually quite spectacular), traffic is routed this way until the mess is cleaned up.

# JEEP RENTALS AND TAXI FARES

## JEEP RENTALS

There are quite a few jeep rental places on St. John. All are located in Cruz Bay, but most have a pickup/drop-off service to the hotels. The rental rates are all just about identical. Stateside discounts and special deals are not honored here. Check with your car insurance company and/or credit card company to see if you are covered for four-wheel drive car rentals. You must be 21 years old or older and have a valid driver's license.

The most inexpensive rentals are 2-door Suzuki's with 4-wheel drive, automatic transmission, and seating (barely) for 4 people. As the passenger capacity goes up so does the price. The largest are the Safari Trucks (long or short bed pickups with benches in the back, usually not 4WD) and the SUV's (which are 4WD).

It may seem like there are a lot of car rental companies for such a small island, but frequently during high season all the cars are rented out. Advance reservations could keep you from being disappointed. (See Update chapter for more on Rental cars).

It is possible but controversial to rent a vehicle on St. Thomas and bring it over on the barge (St. John car renters like their monopoly and fought this very, very hard). The disadvantages to doing this is: the barges only run until about 6:30 pm so you may not be able to get the car over on the same day you fly in; if the car breaks down you are responsible for getting it towed back to St. Thomas; and there are very few four-wheel drive vehicles for rent on St. Thomas.

Here is the list of St. John Car Rental Agencies:
Delbert Hill: (800) 537-6238, (340) 776-6637

Conrad Sutton: (340) 776-6479
Hertz-Varlack Ventures: (340) 693-7580
St. John Car Rental: (340) 776-6103
Cool Breeze: (340) 776-6588
Spencer: (340) 693-8784
Denzil Clyne: (340) 776-6715
Best Car Rental (formerly Budget) (340) 693-8177
Hospitality Car Rental: (340) 693-9160
Avis: (340) 776-6303
Penn's Jeep Rental: (340) 776-6530
O'Conner Jeep Rental: (340) 776-6343
Courtesy Car Rental: (340) 776-6650
C & C Car Rental: (340) 693-8164

## TAXI FARES

These are the official taxi rates for St. John as of the moment, but there may be a "fuel surcharge" in effect. If anyone ever convinces a taxi driver to take them to Zootenvaal or Hurricane Hole, I would really like to know about it. I cannot imagine it ever happening, and certainly not for the price listed here, but they say miracles do happen. These fares are subject to change, all drivers are supposed to post a fare list in their taxi.

| From Cruz Bay To: | Total for 1 person | Total for 2 people | Each for 3 or more |
|---|---|---|---|
| Annaberg | 13.00 | 18.00 | 9.00 |
| Caneel Bay | 6.00 | 10.00 | 5.00 |
| Chocolate Hole | 7.00 | 12.00 | 6.00 |
| Cinnamon Bay | 9.00 | 14.00 | 7.00 |
| Coral Bay | 16.00 | 18.00 | 9.00 |
| Gallows Point | 5.00 | 8.00 | 4.00 |
| Hurricane Hole | 18.00 | 24.00 | 12.00 |
| Maho Bay | 11.00 | 14.00 | 7.00 |
| Reef Bay Trail | 9.00 | 14.00 | 7.00 |
| Salt Pond | 20.00 | 28.00 | 14.00 |
| Trunk Bay | 8.00 | 12.00 | 6.00 |
| Westin Hotel | 6.00 | 10.00 | 5.00 |
| Zootenvaal | 18.00 | 24.00 | 12.00 |

Some taxis also offer a two-hour island tour for about $35 per person.

# PLACES TO STAY

St. John has two large hotels, both luxurious and expensive, numerous condos, two campgrounds, and a few small inns. There are also plenty of vacation villas available on all parts of the island. Another way to visit St. John is to charter a yacht, with or without a captain, and anchor in a different bay every night.

Contact the USVI Department of Tourism at (800) 372-USVI or www.usvitourism.vi for the official accommodations rate sheet, or search the internet for other sites.

St. John has no longer been spared the high-density resort development found on St. Thomas. Most of our mega-projects are still under construction and I do not list them here – nor do I recommend them in any way. In my opinion, they have done a great disservice to St. John and her people just to make a big profit.

## HOTELS

**Caneel Bay Resort,** P.O. Box 720, St. John, VI 00831, Tel. (340) 776-6111 or (800) 338-0487. Caneel Bay is a deluxe resort built on one of the most beautiful peninsulas on St. John. There are seven magnificent white sandy beaches – one for each day of the week, historic ruins from the plantation days, a National Park hiking trail, and a botanist's dream of tropical flowers and plants on the grounds. A number of excellent restaurants are scattered around the complex. The rooms are in small buildings tucked in different corners of the grounds, connected by small courtesy buses. Mr. Rockefeller designed the resort as a hide-a-way, so there are no telephones or TV's in the rooms. Air conditioning is currently being installed, otherwise sea breezes and ceiling fans provide the cooling.

**Westin Resort of St. John,** P.O. Box 8310, St. John, VI 00831, Tel. (340) 693-8000 or (800) 808-5020. The Westin is also a deluxe resort, but more of an American version. The meticulously-groomed grounds look like a movie set, and are maintained *a la* Hollywood – when the plants get too big, they are dug out and replaced with correctly-sized ones. There are all kinds of organized activities, day care for the kids, lots of health-oriented stuff – aerobics, hikes and jogs, exercise classes in the pool, tennis instruction, etc., along with all the regular resort features.

**Gallows Point,** P.O. Box 58, St. John, VI 00831, Tel. (340) 776-6434 or (800) 808-5020. Gallows Point is a five-minute walk to Cruz Bay. It offers one-bedroom luxury suites on the small resort grounds.

## SMALL INNS

**Inn at Tamarind Court,** P.O. Box 350, St. John, VI 00831, Tel. (340) 776-6378 or (800) 221-1637. Tamarind Court has a variety of different-sized rooms with or without bath. The Inn is located in Cruz Bay and has a popular, busy bar and restaurant in the courtyard. Very friendly and helpful staff. Inexpensive.

**St. John Inn,** P.O. Box 37, St. John, VI 00831, Tel. (340) 693-8688 or (800) 666-7688. The St. John Inn located on a small side street in Cruz Bay, has a variety of rooms and apartments, each one different. There is a small pool, an honor bar with superb sunsets.

**Estate Lindholm,** P.O. Box 1360, St. John, VI 00831, Tel. (340) 776-6121 or (800) 322-6335. An intimate bed and breakfast, just outside of Cruz Bay.

**Estate Zootenvaal,** Tel. (340) 776-6321 www.estatezootenvaal.com. Zootenvaal, located on the road to East End, past Coral Bay, is completely surrounded by the National Park, which has protected it from the development frenzy attacking the rest of the island. It offers 1- and 2-bedroom houses on the water in Hurricane Hole. Say Hi for me to the very friendly manager, Robin.

## COTTAGES AND VILLA RENTAL AGENCIES

**Book-It VI,** (340) 693-8555, www.bookitvi.com

**Carefree Getaways on St. John,** (340) 779-4070 or (888) 643-6002, www.carefreegetaways.com

**Caribe Havens,** (340) 776-6518, www.caribehavens.com

**Caribbean Villas,** (800) 338-0987, www.caribbeanvilla.com

**Catered To,** (340) 776-6641 or (800) 424-6641, www.cateredto.com

**Destination St. John,** (340) 779-4647 or (800) 562-1901
www.destinationstjohn.com

**Great Caribbean Getaways,** (340) 693-8692 or (800) 341-2532
www.greatcaribbeangetaways.com

**Island Getaways,** (340) 693-7676 or (888) 693-7676
www.islandgwetawaysinc.com

**Jadan Cottages,** (340) 776-6423

**Samuel Cottages,** (340) 776-6643

**Seaview Vacation Homes,** (340) 776-6805, www.seaviewhomes.com

**Suite St. John,** (340) 776-6969 or (800) 3148-8444, www.suitestjohn.com

**Vacation Vistas,** (340)776-6462, www.vacationvistas.com

**VIVA! Vacations,** (888) 856-4601, www.vivavacations.com

**Windspree,** (340) 693-5423, www.windspree.com

## YACHT CHARTERS

**Admiralty Yacht Vacations,** P.O. Box 306162, St. Thomas, VI 00803
Tel. (340) 774-1376 or (800) 544-0493

**Caribbean Yacht Owners Association,** 5300 Long Bay Road, Yacht Haven, St. Thomas, VI 00802, Tel. (340) 774-3677 or (800) 524-2073

**Caribbean Yacht Charters,** 41-6-1 Frydenhoj, St. Thomas, VI 00803
Tel. (340) 775-6003 or (800) 225-2520

**Island Yachts,** 6100 Red Hook Quarter #4, St. Thomas, VI 00802
Tel. (340) 775-6666 or (800) 524-2019

**Proper Yachts,** P.O. Box 70, St. John, VI 00831
Tel. (340) 776-6256

**Vacations in Paradise** (VIP), P.O. Box 6760, St. Thomas, VI 00804
Tel. (340) 776-1510 or (800) 524-2015

# CAMPGROUNDS

**Cinnamon Bay Campground,** P.O. Box 720, St. John, VI 00831, Tel. (340) 776-6330 or (800) 223-7637. Cinnamon Bay Campground is part of the National Park. This can make it very difficult to get reservations because you have to go through the U.S. National Park Reservation System. There are permanent canvas tents on wood platforms, concrete bungalows, or bare tent sites. There is no swimming pool, but otherwise full resort facilities.

**Maho Bay Campground,** P.O. Box 310, St. John, VI 00831, Tel. (340) 776-6240 or (800) 392-9004. Maho Bay Campground has permanent tents, each with a porch and kitchen area. These delightful units are scattered on a hillside at Maho Bay - the far end of the North Shore Road from Cruz Bay. Full resort facilities except for no swimming pool, and very friendly, fun loving, staff and guests. (See Update chapter for more information on Maho Campground).

**Concordia,** 20-27 Estate Concordia, St. John, VI 00830; Tel: (340) 693-5855 or (800) 392-9004. Concordia offers "eco-tents" with kitchette and bath, or luxury condo units. There is a pool.

**Vie's Campground,** Tel. (340) 693-5033. Very, very basic campground facilities, a long way out on the East End, but with a lovely hostess and beautiful beach. Vie is only open when she wants to be so be sure to call first and make arrangements.

# MAJOR CHANGES SINCE LAST UPDATE

The last complete revision to this book was done in 2009. Here are all of the major changes that have occurred since then.

## OUR INFRASTRUCTURE

You are on St. John, not at home, so do not expect everything to be exactly what you are used to. (Isn't that the point of going on vacation?) We are improving but still have problems with things you may consider basic necessities. Our electricity goes out frequently and you will have to use candles and flashlights. Cable TV constantly has problems, including going off-the-air for long periods of time. If you use too much water the cistern will run dry and you will have to wait for a truck to deliver more. Your hotel or villa may have internet capacity but it too sometimes doesn't work. There are only a few public WiFi hotspots, and none of them are a Starbucks. Cell phone reception is spotty and in some areas completely non-existent. The apps you routinely use to travel around cities and plan routes do not work here. You could embrace this and throw away all electronic devices, including your watch. Inform your boss that it will be impossible for you to check in regularly. Go back to a simpler life.

## CELL PHONES, GPS, AND GOOGLE MAPS

St. John is extremely hilly, which means you will not get cell phone reception on all parts of the island. In fact, you should come expecting NO reception, then can be pleasantly surprised if/when your phone does work (Verizon seems to have the most problems). Most of the North Shore beaches do not have reception, along the Salt Pond Road reception stops at about Shipwreck Restaurant, there are areas of the South Shore that are hidden from a tower, and in many areas your phone will roam and may pick up the Tortola tower which is an international call and costs a fortune! Not being able to count on using your cell means you may have to change your usual patterns and make plans ahead of time since you will not be able to check in constantly like you do at home. Lack of cell phone reception means that your i-Pads won't work either and you will not be able to google something on your i-Phone.

Even if you have reception, GPS and Google Earth-type map resources DO NOT WORK on St. John, because the maps are extremely inaccurate, plus there are problems with incorrect altitude and location readings (even I know that the altitude should be 0 if I am standing on the beach with my toes in the water). The maps are based on the official VI Government Road maps which show any and all roads that have been funded as actually existing – which is completely untrue. Many times money was given out to pave a road (sometimes more than once), yet it never actually happened. However Federal Funds must be accounted for so the VI Government just made the map to show the roads as paved, even though the road may not be even a goat trail. The official Government map also is missing some major paved roads – like the ones that go to Annaberg and Maho Campground, and the road out to Rendezvous and Fish Bay. In addition, Google Earth and others do not know of very many locations on St. John, so you cannot ask for directions to a particular beach or restaurant or neighborhood. The end result is some very crazy suggested routes, for example one program's suggested route from Cruz Bay to Coral Bay was via the L'Esperance Trail – a walking trail that goes to Reef Bay! One man flipped his rental jeep trying to follow instructions from one of the map services. He totaled the rental jeep but his family managed to jump out with only minor bruises and scratches.

Use the regular maps like the ones in this book and rely on your eyes to decide whether a road is safe. Any dirt road can get washed out from a heavy rain, and so can our paved roads. Please use common sense – if it doesn't look like a good road, park and walk.

The very best places to get accurate electronic maps is from the **Trail Bandits website** (www.trailbandit.org). He has great printed maps to buy or you can download many maps for free. For GPS fanatics, he has an extremely accurate GPS map that you can download along with all his coordinates for the official National Park Trails and plenty of unofficial ones for those looking for "Off-the-Trail" hiking adventures.

Google may eventually get more accurate but it is going to be really difficult for a non-official person to convince them that an official Government map shows a two-lane paved road that does not exist. If anyone has a contact with Google maps that could help us get these errors fixed, let me know.

## GAS STATIONS

Currently there is only one gas station functioning on the entire island – **E&C Gas** in Cruz Bay. The Coral Bay Gas station is still closed, but the lawsuit was finally settled last month and the Domino gas folks have to remove the underground tanks by Summer 2013. This will allow a new person to install new tanks and get the gas station up and running again – which is desperately needed. In Cruz Bay, there seems to be a competition for who can try to build a gas station in the most ridiculous location. The winner so far is the St. Thomas company building the gas station near the Westin Hotel on a the steep hill. Incredibly, they have not yet finished excavating down to the required level, the hillside keeps caving in, the massive 35-foot tall retaining walls are failing, and yet construction continues. The latest contender is a site on Centerline Road just a little past Dolphin market, where a local boat captain is excavating and removing the entire hillside to build his gas station, and he will also need massive retaining walls to hold up the sheer cliffs he is creating. Another zoning request was submitted to build a gas station on Centerline Road on a blind curve just at the one end of straight stretch in Susannaberg. That one hasn't been heard from for a while. So until one of these other stations actually opens up, plan ahead and get gas long before you need it – not like my brother who likes to see if he can make one more trip to Coral Bay, then has to borrow my gas can and my car to go back to town because he ran out.

## RENTAL CARS AND THE BARGE

The car rental companies on St. John have finally gotten the VI Government OK to expand the number of cars in their fleet, so beginning in 2013 there should be enough cars to go around in high season now, and maybe, just maybe, the rental rate may go down a little. It is possible (and cheaper) to rent a jeep on St. Thomas and take it on the barge over to St. John – but, if you have any problems it is a long way for them to come fix your vehicle, and if your flight is late, you may miss the last barge and be stuck - either on St. Thomas with nowhere to stay, or on St. John with no way to get to your villa.

## NEW CRUZ BAY PARKING

The VI Government has been promising to resolve the Cruz Bay parking shortage for years and years and years. All kinds of expensive complicated parking garage-type solutions were proposed but never built. Recently, one of our local activists, **Steve Black,** succeeded in convincing the government to create a large, low-cost, desperately-needed, parking lot down by the tennis courts and the barge dock. It is a short 5-minute walk to the Cruz Bay restaurants and shops. This area is the remnants of a salt pond left over from building the barge dock facility. All that was needed was a bulldozer to push the dirt into the center, then various types of material and gravel were used to build up and compact the earth so the cars wouldn't sink. It was done quickly and cheaply and we use it all the time. Thanks Steve.

## HONEYMOON BEACH AND CANEEL

Caneel Resort has now established a snack bar, bathrooms, and a beach toy rental concession at Honeymoon Beach. This concession was quite a surprise since in recent years, Caneel has made it very clear that they have absolutely no interest in visitors or (even worse) locals visiting their property. Then we discovered the concessionaire is a St. Thomas company and caters primarily to the day sailboats coming over from St. Thomas rather than to people arriving via the Lind Point Trail, and has opening hours that match that of the day charters.

The community is not happy with Caneel's new anti-visitor policies and does not understand why the National Park, who owns and is in charge of the Caneel Property, has done nothing to stop Caneel from making up new rules limiting non-guests from using the National Park trails and beaches. Caneel is now charging a $20 parking fee for visitors and they have completely restricted access to the Turtle Point Trail – which is an official National Park Trail. They will however take your money if you want to shop in their gift shop, or the restaurant or bar. At the moment, you can park on the North Shore Road and walk to Caneel Beach and then on to Honeymoon and Solomon beaches, but there are reports of some people being told that they could not come in by foot. If you are arriving from the Lind Point Trail, they haven't figured out how to stop you yet, and no one can stop you from going to any beach via the water. So you can rent one of those kayaks and go to Turtle Point Beach or Scott Beach, or any of the other Caneel beaches.

## HANDICAP ACCESSIBLE TRAILS

Wooden boardwalks have been installed at both the Cinnamon Bay Ruins and a portion of the Francis Bay Nature Trail, so more people can enjoy these facilities. Please understand that St. John welcomes handicapped people, but it is a physically difficult place, with lots of the steep hills and dirt roads, causing access difficulties for everyone, and especially so for those with handicaps.

## PARKING LOT AT MAHO BAY BEACH

The National Park has finally provided more parking at one beach – Maho Bay. At the farthest end of the beach from Cruz Bay is a parking lot. It would be nice if they ever finished it off a little bit more, but it serves the purpose. Now if they would do the same for the rest of the beaches.

## MAHO CAMPGROUND

Maho Campground's long term lease expired a few years ago and they have been operating on 1-year extensions since then while the owners try to find a buyer for the property. The latest news is that there is a serious prospective buyer and the campground will have to close in May 2013. But we have heard that before, so I am not willing to erase them off the map just yet. Attempts by organizations to buy and preserve the land by donating it to the National Park have failed so far. Mr. Selegut has no desire to purchase the property himself (although he is hoping someone else will buy it and give it to him to continue running the campground on it). Instead he has concentrated on moving his Maho operation over to his other property near Salt Pond – **Concordia Eco Resorts.**

## CONCORDIA ECO-RESORT GROWING

With Maho almost closing, Concordia has been expanding in size and volume of guests. This has resulted in an increase in traffic on the roads and on the beaches around the Salt Pond area. Campers jog to Ram Head in the morning, Drunk Bay sculptors have very little room left to be creative until after a storm wipes the place clean, and the sandy beaches – Salt Pond and Little Lameshur are getting more crowded throughout the year.

And it finally happened: two of the bays I have kept "secret" must now be deemed discovered and added to my maps. Both of these bays are NOT in the National Park and you have to go through private subdivisions to get to them. Please be respectful of the neighborhood. **Kiddle Bay** and **Grootpan Bay** are rocky beaches located down a rutted dirt road that is currently in OK shape but can get impassable even with four-wheel drive vehicles. To find these bays, turn left onto a dirt road just past the Salt Pond Parking lot. It is a very bumpy road that winds around a hill then eventually comes back out to the main road again – a big loop. There is a T-intersection at the point farthest from the road – go left to get to the bays. For Kiddle, turn left again, but beware!!! This road can be very difficult to navigate even with good four-wheel drive skills. Park and walk or send a scout down on foot if you are not sure of the conditions. For Grootpan Bay go straight a little more then turn right down a very bad dirt road. You may scratch the car – be careful.

## BORDEAUX MOUNTAIN ROAD PAVING

The Bordeaux Mountain Road is now paved almost the entire way with just a small section of clay road left unfinished. The clay is extremely difficult to pave and is pretty hard to drive on when wet, but you can usually make it with four-wheel drive. The very, very steep hill coming up from Coral Bay is paved, but you will still need four-wheel drive when the road is even slightly wet. While this is major progress for St. John, it still does not count as an alternative route into Coral Bay because trucks, which are necessary to provide water, food, garbage, beer and everything else to Coral Bay, still cannot make it up the hill – it is too steep.

## CORAL BAY RESTAURANTS AND MARINAS

Restaurants come and go, change names and owners so often that I don't bother trying to list them all here. But there are a few that are landmarks that need to be mentioned. **Pickles Deli** in Coral Bay has just reopened after 10 years of being gone and it is just the same. An option to buy has been placed on the Cocolobo Complex, Voyages, Island Blues, B&B, and Cases by the Sea area of Coral Bay, by a developer intending to build a very high-end deluxe marina. Marinas have been proposed before in Coral Bay and the EPA always says the same thing – no dredging. Since the water is barely 3-feet deep, this makes any marina for more than a rowboat pretty impossible to build, but developers have pulled off other miracles so we will wait and see. If that happens, all of that area will change drastically. On the other side of Coral Bay, that very large marina, condo, hotel, resort proposal has been put on hold.

## HANSEN BAY BEACH ACCESS

There is a family estate battle happening out in East End near Miss Vie. The end result is Vie's Campground has been fenced off and access to that section of beach is now found further down the road just before the derelict white building. The sign is a little confusing, but means it is OK for you to use this path as access to the beach, just be aware that the campground inside the fence is private property. Across from the campground gate is the dirt road traditionally used to walk to Newfound Bay. This road has been closed to the public by some family members and the case is now in Courts for resolution.

## NEW CORAL IS GROWING

In 2005, 50% of our coral reefs died due to the water temperature getting so high it stressed and weakened the coral so that they could not fight off diseases. The big question was what will happen now? Will all the coral die, will the reefs adapt, will the fish die? Well, the coral is growing back – quite rapidly. There are brand new elkhorn colonies scattered around, pillar coral appears to be adding on encrusting duties to its vertical columns, many soft corals are expanding into areas where the hard coral has died, and other different species are moving onto the dead coral. The fish are still here but are now threatened by the introduction of the South Pacific lionfish, which eats tremendous amounts of reef fish and has no predators in this part of the world. Even more exciting, our mangrove lagoons are thriving with hard and soft coral, sponges, baby fish, baby lobsters, anemones, and all kinds of other critters. Our local marine biologist **Caroline Rogers,** has recently begun studying the mangroves and she was surprised to find mangrove corals are far healthier than the coral found on reefs, and was stunned by the diversity of species. Check out the excellent photographs in her latest book *The Mysterious Magical Mangroves of St. John.*

## ST. JOHN HERMIT CRABS ARE FAMOUS!

In August 2012, I happened to be in the right place at the right time to see a massive **Solder Crab** (a/k/a Hermit Crab) **migration** – a river of literally millions of crabs heading into the sea. The river was about 100 feet wide and the crabs were over one foot deep – walking on top of each other. I called photographer **Steve Simonsen** and told him to drop everything and come right away. He did and filmed this amazing event, set it to music, and put it out on the Internet. It went viral – millions of hits. The crabs were shown on Good Morning America, on the Smithsonian home page, on lots of news shows. We got calls from Nature magazine, National Geographic, and from biologists around the world. It was amazing and deservedly so – the video is extraordinary. Google **"St. John Crab Video"** and watch it for yourself.

I had heard about these crab migrations but had never seen one. The story I was told was that crabs came down from the hills sometime in August, took off their shells, jumped into the sea, had crazy sex, came back out of the water, put on a new shell and went back up the mountain. So when I grabbed my snorkel gear and jumped into the water I expected to see millions of naked crabs, but there was no nudity at all. The crabs stayed in their shells, went into the water until it was about 1 foot deep, then reached around and grabbed fertilized eggs and flung them into the sea. OK, so that meant all of the crabs were female. Did this mean the orgy happened on the beach, not in the water? Nope. I found out that it takes a few weeks after sex for the eggs to be mature enough to release. So what really happens is the guys and girls get together up in the hills, do the deed, then he stays there relaxing (smoking a cigarette maybe) while she makes the long trek down to the beach, goes into the water, releases her eggs, then hikes back up the hill. This turns out to be a very fast process. The entire going into the water portion of the migration was over in about 6 hours. I checked the next day and there were only a handful of crabs left still working their way up the hill. All those millions had disappeared in less than 24 hours.

As you can see in the video, all of these crabs were the same size, it was like a high school reunion for just one class. I verified that very unusual scene and no one can explain why there were so many crabs of the same age in one little St. John watershed. Maybe the Concordia resort expansion is providing so much food the crab population has exploded? Another mystery.

I asked around to see if any other St. John beaches had a crab migration that same day – none had been seen. So it is not like coral where all of them spawn on the same day, and does not seem to be linked to the moon phase. And in late October I saw another migration (I am becoming a crab magnet) so it is not limited to the month of August. All of this is why biologists have very little data about this migration – it takes place very quickly and at no predictable time and although certain beaches are known as crab beaches, not every beach is used every year.

As you can see, I am completely fascinated about the crab migration, and Steve and I have made plans for next year. We have set up a crab hotline – if you see a large amount of crabs crossing the road or in the bushes on a beach, send an email to **crabs@pamgaffin.com** with details of how many crabs, where exactly did you see them and when exactly (time/date). If the whole island and all the visitors are looking out for crabs we should be able to see more migrations and collect more information on how all of this works – and of course Steve will get more wonderful video material.

## YELLOWFOOTED TORTOISES

My sister feels that I have done an injustice to the Yellowfooted Tortoises in this book and that I need to provide more information about them, so here goes. These South American natives were brought to St. John by early visitors (like the Tainos and Arawaks) who worked their way up the Caribbean island chain by canoe. Along with some large rodents which are now extinct, the tortoises were brought here and released to provide a food source for future visits. Later on the Europeans did the same thing with deer and boar. These are land tortoises – not water turtles, and as their name says they have red spots on their feet and head and yellow spots on their shells. They can grow to be over 18 inches long and take two hands to pick. The tortoises are found primarily in the dry part of St. John around John's Folly and Estate Quacco Zimmerman. Occasionally they are seen in other parts of the island – if you see them on the road, stop and move them out of harm's way please. They are extremely intelligent and very curious. Mine know their names, come when they are called, will "jump" over a 4 x 4 on command, and love playing with people, especially the bulldozer game where they push chairs and anything else all over the deck. All of my house sitters think they are going to enjoy my cats and end up falling in love with my tortoises instead, while my cats refuse to acknowledge their existence. Animal rights folks – please note my tortoises are not being held as prisoners. They can leave whenever they want, but since one has always lived in captivity and the two others are blind and crippled, they choose to stay and have me provide them with food, water, and entertainment.

## ROAD HAZARDS: DONKEYS, DEER, IGUANAS AND SHEEP

In recent years, St. John has been very fortunate in dodging hurricanes and avoiding droughts. This means the vegetation has been thriving, making our island very green, and also has allowed our animal population to thrive. Deer used to be very shy and afraid of people, but now that no one is hunting them, they are getting bold and you may encounter them on the roads which can be very dangerous especially at night. The Iguana population has exploded and they also cross the road without looking both ways, and are especially stupid during mating season in the spring. The donkeys have recently learned they are cute and developed a successful business getting tourists to stop along the roads and feed them in exchange for photographs. They will stick their heads into your car looking for handouts and if in a group, there can be some aggressive pushing and jostling to be the one to get fed. These donkeys are not owned by anyone, so you are welcome to take one home with you. On the Coral Bay side, the goat population has finally been reduced, but now the sheep herd owner has become completely irresponsible (he has a girlfriend in the Dominican Republic so is not here very much). Frequently, the herd completely blocks the roads; just beep your horn and push through slowly, they will get out of the way of your car. Our goats and sheep look almost identical. The way to tell the difference is: tail up is a goat, tail down is a sheep.

## ST. JOHN HISTORICAL SOCIETY WEBSITE

The St. John Historical Society has accumulated a great deal of historical information, photos, books, and other collections documenting the historic and cultural heritage of St. John. They have not yet found a building for a museum, but they have set up a wonderful website. There is an extensive photo collection, plus a library of articles and presentations. If you are interested in this aspect of St. John, please check it out at www.stjohnhistoricalsociety.org.

## PYRAMID APPEARS IN CRUZ BAY PARK

Directly across the street from the ferry dock, at the entrance of the park in Cruz Bay is a pyramid. It is supposed to have the name of the park – Frank Powell Park – on it. But all of the letters didn't fit so they took them down after being up for the Governor's one-day visit. There was a perfectly good sign identifying the park, it was taken down and four men worked for a week to construct this pyramid. No one can explain why a pyramid was chosen, it has nothing to do with St. John or Virgin Islands culture and we are a long way from Egypt. Kids like to climb on it (and some adults) and it meshed well with one person's Cleopatra Halloween costume, but otherwise we are all mystified by it.

## L'ESPERANCE TRAIL IS OFFICIAL

Just as I was sending this edition off to the printer, a new National Park sign appeared for the L'Esperance Trail! No one is exactly sure how this former Trail Bandit trail became officially sanctioned by the Park, just like no one is sure who exactly decided to "de-sanction" the Turtle Point Trail at Caneel Bay. But there is now a sign on Centerline Road showing distances to the ruins (.3 mile), the Great Sieben Trail leading to the baobab tree and Fish Bay (1.0), the Reef Bay Sugar Mill ruins and Genti Beach (2.6).

# INDEX

To order American Paradise Publishing books, please see our website at www.AmericanParadisePublishing.com or write to PO Box 781, St. John, VI 00831 or email info@AmericanParadisePublishing.com.

**St. John People** by various St. John authors                    **$20.00**
Twenty profiles of contemporary St. John residents written by a
dozen St. John writers. This book is a fascinating journey straight
into the heart of contemporary St. John.
ISBN 0-9631060-5-8 (230 pages, illustrated)

**St. John: Feet, Fins & 4-Wheel Drive** by Pam Gaffin           **$15.00**
A complete guide to St. John driving, swimming, and hiking.
Revised in 2009. Reprinted with update in 2013.
ISBN 0-9631060-9-0 (152 pages, with numerous maps)


# ST. JOHN: FEET, FINS & FOUR WHEEL DRIVE
## AUTHOR OFFERS GUIDE SERVICE

Pam Gaffin, author of this book, is now available to take visitors hiking, snorkeling and touring. Tell me what you are interested in and I will custom design a tour suited to your interests and abilities (we could even go to "secret" places that are not in this book!). Extreme hike/snorkels are a specialty. Only nice people please – no whiners. See **www.PamGaffin.com** for details.